OPTIONS IN CONTEMPORARY THEOLOGY

Stanley T. Sutphin

UNIVERSITY
PRESS OF
AMERICA

Copyright © 1977 by

University Press of America, Inc.™

P.O. Box 19101, Washington, D.C. 20036

ISBN (Perfect): 0-8191-0277-6

ACKNOWLEDGEMENTS

The author of Options in Contemporary Theology is
grateful to the following for permission to reprint
copyrighted materials:
Association Press, New York, for an excerpt from
   William Hamilton's The New Essence of Christianity;
The Christian Century Foundation, Chicago, for an
   excerpt from "Seminarian, Meet Theologian," by
   Hugh T. Kerr. Copyright 1975 Christian Century
   Foundation. Reprinted by permission from the
   February 5-12, 1975 issue of The Christian Century;
Harper & Row Publishers, Inc., New York, for an excerpt
   from Sam Keen's To a Dancing God; for an excerpt
   from Martin Heidegger's Being and Time;
Harvard University Press, Cambridge, for an excerpt
   from Harvey Cox's The Feast of Fools, Harvard
   University Press, 1969;
John Knox Press, Atlanta, for an excerpt from Martin
   Heidegger by John Macquarrie. Used by permis-
   sion of the publisher, John Knox Press;
J. B. Lippincott Company Publishers, New York, for an
   excerpt from A Black Theology of Liberation by
   James H. Cone. Copyright © 1970 by James H.
   Cone. Reprinted by permission of J. B. Lippin-
   cott Company;
Northwestern University Press, Evanston, for an excerpt
   from The Primacy of Perception: And Other Essays
   on Phenomenological Psychology, the Philosophy of
   Art, History and Politics, by Maurice Merleau-
   Ponty, edited by James M. Edie, Northwestern
   University Press, 1964; for an excerpt from
   Husserl: An Analysis of His Phenomenology, by Paul
   Ricoeur, trans. by Edward G. Ballard and Lester
   E. Embree, Northwestern University Press, 1967; for
   an excerpt from History and Truth, by Paul Ricoeur,
   trans. by Charles A. Kelbley, Northwestern Univer-
   sity Press, 1965;
Orbis Books, Maryknoll, NY, for an excerpt from A
   Theology of Liberation, by Gustavo Gutierrez,
   trans. and edited by Caridad Inda and John
   Eagleson;
Philosophical Library, Inc., New York, for an excerpt
   from Being and Nothingness: An Essay on Phenomenological Ontology, by Paul Sartre, trans. by Hagel
   E. Barnes;

Contents

INTRODUCTION

Genuine faith, because it involves the whole person, has always driven people to consider its total implications for life. Theology has been the discipline in the Judaeo-Christian tradition which has endeavored to express and clarify the hopes and understandings of the community of the faithful regarding its faith and beliefs. The term "theology" literally means a rational thought or word about God (Theos, the Greek term for God, and logos, meaning word or rational thought). The theologian has been the person who has traditionally tried to organize and articulate this "word" in such a manner as to make it generally clear and convincing to each succeeding generation of the faithful.

From earliest times theologians have recognized that their listeners, at whom their discourses on the meaning of the faith were directed, were basically of two minds -- those who constituted the core of the faith community and those who stood looking in from the periphery. Those theologians whose listeners were made up essentially of the hard-core faithful tended to speak authoritatively about the belief structures of the faith and this branch of theologizing assumed the characteristics of dogmatizing about revealed truths. However, in contrast to this kind of theologizing, which eventually became designated as Dogmatic theology, there have always been those theologians who stood with one foot in the faith community and one foot in the philosophical and intellectual world of their times and who have tried sincerely to find a common ground for discourse. By the second century of the Christian era this latter group of theologians came to be referred to as Apologists (an apology was originally understood as a defense a man made before a court). The apologist did not assume that the truths of the faith community were self-evident. He tried to find new and meaningful ways of interpreting the faith, and its belief structures, to those who either criticized or doubted its veracity. Over the centuries this style of theologizing has been designated as Natural theology and in more recent times it has been called simply philosophical theology.

While there has been a long history during which theologians tried to make a sharp distinction between dogmatic and apologetic theology, such a sharp distinction has never been completely justified. Dogmatic theology has always presupposed certain philosophical elements -- the nature of reality which all men experience, what constitutes rational procedure such as deduction, linguistic meanings, etc. -- whereas, apologetic or natural theology has always begun with a faith assumption. Indeed, recently a long-time, distinguished professor of theology at Princeton Theological Seminary, and editor of Theology Today, Hugh T. Kerr, declared that in the 1970s he tended to "think of theology more as art than philosophy, more as a critical perspective than a bundle of beliefs, more symbolic than discursive, more pluralistic than dogmatic or apologetic."[1] (Italics mine) Perhaps this description of Kerr's comes closer to the way in which theologians see the task of theologizing today rather than in the traditional dogmatic-apologetic framework. Nevertheless, while the kinds of theology which is examined in this book as representative of the various contemporary options in theology fulfill many if not all of the features which Kerr mentions, still, there is a decided apologetic character in all of them. Perhaps this simply means that the theologian of the late twentieth century has very little option but to do apologetic theology. The waves of pluralism and skepticism which have swept across America in the last decade have become the normative context in which theology must be done. From this writer's perspective all theology that is worth its salt today must take on the characteristics of justifying or defending the faith, either under the standard of relevancy or that of intellectual respectability and compatibility.[2]

What has brought about this apparent shift in the theological approach of the 1970s? Most theological observers seem to agree that America is feeling the impact of that which is succinctly called "secularism."[3] Secularism characterizes a general mood, attitude and value system which is frequently designated as a radical "this-worldliness." Its stress is on the temporal, the here-and-now, the immediate, the sensate of this world of space and time. It affirms that all things are relative, mortal, conditioned, and finite. It holds that nature and humankind are the results of contingency forces which are neither rational, necessary, nor purposive. It asserts the self-determination of each person along with the relativity and pluralism of all values.

Secularism is a general mood which has paralleled certain objective transformations in the social and institutional cultural patterns of the modern age. Certainly the scientific and technological engineering of the human world, its institutions -- the church, state, class, and family, makes people certain that these institutions are no longer under the control of some transcendent power which must be obeyed. Rather, secular persons know that the environment is the product of geographical and natural forces, of human efforts and power structures, which are essentially of their own making. Secular people believe that what is real in this universe is a strange interaction of a somewhat fortuitous benevolent nature and the blind forces of matter, which produce the temporary social institutions in which they live, create artifacts, patterns of relationships, and relative values. Any notion of a "transcendent" or "sacred" realm of being for the secularist appears more as a fantasy than it does as a God. Secular people believe that they have "come of age" in a blind, faceless universe. Any notion of an ultimate order, or Orderer, in which meaning or purpose appears has vanished completely for secular people.

While theological reactions to the rising tide of secularism in this country has been taking place over a long period of time, the climax of this reaction occurred in the mid-sixties. At that time a crisis of faith seems to have taken place rather dramatically both within and outside the ecclesiastical community. Despite the many frustrations, guilt, anxiety, and growing international problems of the post-World War II era, Americans still experienced considerable optimism about their culture and their role in history. So long as they appeared to have a booming economy and a strong military force placed strategically throughout the world, Americans believed that they could somehow learn to live with the threat of a nuclear holocaust. Fortuitous for that period of history in the 1940s and 1950s, there was a bevy of brilliant theological minds (Barth, Brunner, Bultmann, Tillich, the Niebuhr brothers, and Buber and Heschel in the Jewish tradition) whose powerful affirmations of the God of revelation and whose creative analyses of the human situation seemed to be capable of carrying people across the chasm of despair. However, even then the chief apologist in the Protestant camp, Paul Tillich, recognized the growing threat of a "godless" culture, when in his work The Courage to Be (1952) he talked about the "God above the God of theism."[4] Nevertheless, the power of these theological giants gave theology in the 1950s not only a useful, meaningful language, but a program of substance and integrity for reflecting upon God and human destiny. The imaginative assimilation of Biblical, historical, secular, and cultural sources into their theological works brought men like Reinhold Niebuhr and Tillich a degree of respect even from the most sophisticated secularist.

The ascending cultural mood for most people during the latter part of the 1950s and the early 1960s, however, was that of secularism. The notion that people needed faith in a transcendent being in order to cope with the problems with which life confronted them was finding less and less support among Americans in the early 1960s. Theologians, spurred on by some of the puzzling, provocative statements of Dietrich Bonhoeffer in his Letters and Papers from Prison,[5] began to write explicitly about the "Death of God" as a cultural fact. Gabriel Vahanian who deserves much credit for pointing out the secular nature of the American culture published a book in 1961 entitled The Death of God.[6] Although Vahanian insisted that the categories and symbols of transcendence, especially those pertaining to God, were no longer relevant and useful to Americans and that God is dead in this age and in this culture, he, personally, did not theologically approve of the secularization of religion. However, William Hamilton, who became one of the outspoken advocates for the "Death of God" theology published a book in the same year in which he wrote: "To be a Christian today is to stand, somehow, as a man without God, but with hope,"[7] Upon his return from Berlin, Germany, Harvey Cox, very much impressed with the spirit of Bonhoeffer, wrote his very popular work The Secular City. Cox argued that the historical basis for the secular world could be found in the Bible and that the secularity of the present age was a good and healthy situation which should be supported and which offered Christianity unusual opportunities.[8] Paradoxically, this did not lead Cox to a secularization of Biblical theology as it did in the cases of William Hamilton, Thomas Altizer, and Paul van Buren.

For Hamilton, Altizer, and van Buren the secular culture's eclipse of God meant that the theologian to be relevant to the age must, likewise, do theology with-

4

out the "hypothesis" of God. Consequently, for a brief
period of time in the mid-sixties the American society
witnessed the strange phenomenon of theologians endeavoring to write and do theology minus the concept of
God. (Which would appear to be analogous to a physicist trying to do physics without the concept of mass)

Very briefly stated, Altizer argues that the
transcendent God of the Bible entered human flesh in
the person of Christ and died as the transcendent,
separate God. Humankind must now await the emergence
of a new deity, or sense of the sacred. The theologians' task, therefore, is to teach people to let go
of the dead God of history and to look for an emergence
of the sacred in some other way.[9] Hamilton seems to be
completely overwhelmed by the cultural mood of secularism and declares that the God of Biblical-Augustinian-
Reformed tradition is no longer real or meaningful for
him either in an objective or subjective sense. God as
a "problem-solver" or "need-fulfiller" is dead and man
must solve his problems and meet his needs without the
notion of a transcendent Being. The task of the theologian, therefore, is (curiously) discovering the role
Jesus would take in the world and "becoming Jesus," or
"unmasking" that role, for Christians.[10] Both Hamilton
and van Buren focus upon the centrality of Jesus as ex-
emplifying the attitude and way of love which is demanded of Christians. Both focus upon his historical
personage. For Paul van Buren the real problem of
Christianity is its religious language. Specifically,
"God" language should be dropped by Christians because
there is no objective, empirical way to verify what
"God-statements" mean. The task of the theologian is
to clarify the essential message of the New Testament
without such references. The picture which the New
Testament sets forth of Jesus is that of a remarkably
"free man" whose freedom from all the normal anxieties
and fears of life make it possible for him to live for
his neighbor, to give himself freely to others. It is
this "freedom" which is so "contagious," asserts van
Buren, that as the Apostle Paul declares others are
"grasped" by it and experience "grace "[11]

The shock effect which these "death of God" theologians had upon both the culture and the ecclesiastical community was rather dramatic. While the public
media -- popular weekly journals, newspapers, radio,
and television -- headlined the phrase "God is dead"

and rushed to expose the spokesmen of these views for a brief period of time, it soon moved on to other realms of public interests. While the immediate reactions of many ministers and popular religious presses were renunciations of the statements and ideas of these theologians, the more serious thinkers within the ecclesiastical communities began to assess the veracity and implications of these radical theological positions. When honest and sensitive men assert that God has been crowded out of the world of human experience, that the Biblical vision of the love of God is contradicted by the vast evil apparent in the world, and that the Biblical notion of God threatens human dignity and freedom, theologians must take notice.[12]

Basically, the "death of God" theologians, who were riding the crest of a strong wave of secularism, affirmed with the dominant cultural mood of that time that: God is dead! Humankind is on its own and in full control of the situation. Therefore, there is no longer any need to speak of "God," especially as One who creates, sustains, governs, and redeems the world. It is sufficient for theologians to speak only of a sense of moral and ethical responsibility for which is found a very adequate model in Jesus of Nazareth.

Looking back over the events of the past decade it would appear that no sooner had these viewpoints been expressed and affirmed by the secularist theologian than they were in the process of being negated. The self-sufficiency of American culture begins to look doubtful when viewed against the background of the prolonged war in Southeast Asia, the mounting ecological crises of a greedy technological mentality, the crumbling pragmatic morality of big business and big government, the increased tensions of a society ravished by continuing spying, lying, assassinations, inequities, and violations of human rights and needs.

The efforts of the secularist theologian to develop a Christian theology without God was a failure. However, the question which they posed about the "unreality of God" remains very much a problem with which theologians must come to terms in an age in which faith in absolutes have vanished. Contemporary theology must deal with the problem of ultimacy, of final meaning and purpose in the human experience, if it is to fulfill its responsible tasks.

The problem confronting the contemporary theologian is actually one of credibility. What human experience, or experiences, within the Western cultural context, prompt people to affirm transcendent values as plausible? What analysis, or what approach to the structures of being, or what perspective on the phenomena of the human community and its environs will convince people that it is more credible to affirm ultimacy than to deny it? What within the context of late twentieth century Western human experience points to the credibility of "faith in God?" What human phenomena convinces people of "God's reality?" The theological perspectives reviewed in this book appear to be, to this writer, the major options to date in the search for an answer to these questions.

[1]Hugh T. Kerr, "Seminarian, Meet Theologian,"
The Christian Century (February 5-12, 1975), p. 106.
[2]Support for this contention that theology must
be of an apologetic nature today can be found in an
article by Ted Peters, "Truth in History: Gadamer's
Hermeneutics and Pannenberg's Apologetic Method,"
The Journal of Religion, Vol. 55 (January, 1975), 36-
56. Peters makes the following statement: "Christian theology is the reflective interpretation of the
witness of Holy Scripture to the reality of God through
Jesus Christ within a particular situation, and for
that interpretation to be adequate it must evolve out
of a genuine 'intellectual discussion' with the prevailing understanding of reality in that situation.
Thus, theology is inescapably apologetic." 36.
[3]Compare, for example, the extensive analysis
of Langdon Gilkey, Naming the Whirlwind: The Renewal
of God-Language (The Bobbs-Merrill Company, 1969),
Part I, chs. 1, 2, and 3, on the cultural and theological background for the current theological situation. Compare, also, Harvey Cox, The Secular City
(The Macmillan Company, 1965), Part One, chs. 1-5;
Sam Keen, Apology For Wonder (Harper & Row, 1969),
chs. IV, V; and Theodore Roszak, The Making of a
Counter Culture (Doubleday & Company, Inc., 1969),
for a non-theological perspective. See, also, two
more recent articles in The Christian Century. Win-
throp S. Hudson, "Reflections on the Meandering Career
of Recent Protestant Theology," The Christian Century
(September 6, 1972), pp. 868-871; Peter L. Berger,
Cakes for the Queen of Heaven: 2,500 Years of Religious
Ecstasy," The Christian Century (December 25, 1974),
pp. 1217-1223, esp., pp. 1220-21.
[4](Yale University Press, 1952), pp. 182-190.
[5]See, for example, Letters and Papers from Prison,
ed. by Eberhard Bethge, tr. by Reginald H. Fuller (Revised Edition: The Macmillan Company, 1967), pp. 168,
187-8.
[6](George Braziller, 1961).
[7]The New Essence of Christianity (Association
Press, 1961), p. 64.
[8]See The Secular City (The Macmillan Company,
1965), pp. 21-36.
[9]See, especially, Altizer's three articles which
are included in the book which he wrote with William
Hamilton, Radical Theology and the Death of God (The

Bobbs-Merrill Company, 1966), "America and the Future of Theology," "Theology and the Death of God," and "The Sacred and the Profane: A Dialectical Understanding of Christianity." See, also, his book The Gospel of Christian Atheism (The Westminster Press, 1966).

[10]See, especially, Altizer and Hamilton, Radical Theology and the Death of God, pp. 35-42, 49-50, and Hamilton's article "Thursday's Child." Also, see his recent article in The Christian Century (October 8, 1975), pp. 872-73, entitled, "In Piam Memoriam -- The Death of God After Ten Years."

[11]See his, The Secular Meaning of the Gospel (The Macmillan Company, 1963), esp., chs. IV, V, and VI.

[12]A very helpful book written primarily for the lay-man and novice theologian is Thomas W. Ogletree's, The Death of God Controversy (Abingdon Press, 1966). This book is an excellent introduction to the background setting for the movement and gives the differences, similarities, and essential theological positions of the three major figures. A very helpful collection of essays covering the background and continuing discussion of the issues raised by the movement can be found in the book Radical Theology: Phase Two Essays in a Continuing Debate (J. B. Lippincott Company, 1967), edited by C. W. Christian and Glenn R. Wittig. The most scholarly assessment of the whole movement and its implications for contemporary theology is to be found in Part I, of Langdon Gilkey's book, op. cit., n. 3 above.

CHAPTER ONE

Cultural or Story Theology

There is a kind of faddishness to what is here being identified as "Cultural" or "Story" theology which makes it somewhat difficult to characterize. In one sense Cultural Theology seems to be almost exclusively concerned with the most current mood or popular notions of Western culture. In this respect it reflects many of the concerns which fostered the "death of God" movement — an ultra-sensitivity to the secular spirit or feelings of the time. There is the same stress on the relativity of ideologies, the significance of the here-and-now, the this-wordly orientation, the sensate, the urban-dependency and scientific-dependency of man's being which was found among the advocates of the death-of-God school of thought in the 1960s. However, the differences are significant in that the cultural theologian appears to have a more balanced understanding of the persistence of the structures of evil and corruption in the human situation and perhaps, a broader appreciation of the importance of the notion of the sacred in man's societies.

Nevertheless, there is a certain peripheral, "pop-like," or anti-intellectual quality about Cultural (or Story) Theology which makes a concise definition almost impossible. The men who write such theology appear to be men who, despite their years of mastering the formal disciplines and the erudition required in the esteemed halls of academe, are more interested in writing a "best seller" than in working out a reasonably defensible theological position.[1] There is a great deal of skill, charm, and wisdom displayed in their writings, but there is a deficiency displayed in the substance of their works. Their concern seems to be more with locating a spiritual and intellectual posture for tomorrow than in finding something reasonably solid for today. Yet because of their interest and concern with the Christian faith, and their much broader faith in the value of religion in general, these men must be considered as apologetic theologians. They are concerned with pointing out the "relevance" of religion in general, if not Christianity in particular, for twentieth-century Western man.

There are a number of theologians whose books and
the substance of which seem to fall into what is clas-
sified in this chapter as Cultural or Story Theology.
The more popular works which appear in the early 19-
70s and whose titles are very suggestive of the theme
are: Harvey Cox, The Feast of Fools: A Theological
Essay on Festivity and Fantasy (1969); Sam Keen, To
a Dancing God (1970); Barry Wood, The Magnificent
Frolic (1970); Michael Novak, Ascent of the Mountain,
Flight of the Dove (1971); and David Miller, Gods and
Games (1971). More recently Cox and Miller have come
through again with eye-catching numbers like The Seduction of the Spirit: The Use and Misuse of People's Religion (1973) and The New Polytheism: Rebirth of the
Gods and Goddesses (1974).

Without a doubt the most popular, prestigious representative of this group of Cultural or Story Theologians is the Harvard Professor Harvey Cox. Since the
publication of his classic best seller The Secular City
(1965), Cox has maintained his search for the avant-
garde theological position. His methodology, which is
typical of the cultural or story theologian, makes use
of a variety of perspectives and disciplines such as
personal biography and experience, sociology, phenomenology, history, symbolic analysis, comparative religions, ecumenical understanding, scientific technology, and theology.[2] As a master synthesizer of many
of the theological tendencies in contemporary religious
life Cox makes an especially good focal point for this
presentation of cultural or story theology. Before
looking at his work, however, brief mention should be
made of the recent theological efforts of Michael Novak
and Sam Keen whose ideas are often reflected by Cox.

NOVAK

Novak, a former Assistant Professor in the Special
Program in the Humanities at Stanford University, Stanford, California, and presently the distinguished
Watson-Ledden professor of religion at Syracuse University, in New York, has been one of the most popular
American Catholic theologians in the past decade. The
author of numerous books, Novak holds degrees from
Harvard University and the Gregorian University in
Rome. At least two of his publications in the latter
part of the 1960s (Vietnam: Crisis of Conscience [1967]
and A Theology For Radical Politics [1969])[3] should have

11

served public notice that Novak was among the avant-garde theologians. However, in Ascent of the Mountain, Flight of the Dove he leaves no doubt about this stance.

Novak declares that the purpose of Ascent of the Mountain, Flight of the Dove is to entice the reader to take a "voyage of self-discovery" in which he will become conscious of his own sense of reality, his own symbols and religious story. Novak contends that he learned long ago that "genuine theology" is "shown" rather than proclaimed and that he, therefore, is offering students the tools for discerning the various ways in which people of other cultures live out different stories using different symbols or different understandings of reality.[4] While the following out of a personal or communal voyage with its emphasis upon experience, self-reflection, and imagination is not the approach of "objective" western scholarship, it is a mode of religious inquiry which enjoys a long tradition among the Hindu, Buddhist, Shinto, and Muslim cultures. And Novak finds very compatible the somewhat anti-intellectual notion that the purpose of study is not to know but to help man to live. Therefore, the creative challenge to the theologian is to displace the conceptual theology of the head with a vision of action (or story). Man does not live primarily by principles but by stories.[5]

Novak lifts up most of the themes with which the cultural or story theologian is concerned such as: a sense of balance between the Dionysiac (the sensual experience, the ecstatic, the enthusiastic) and the Apollonian (the rational, the disciplined, the orderly) man; the fallacy of separating earthly life from spiritual life; the notion that religion is basically a conversion to a sense of the sacred; that religion is the telling of a story with a person's life which unites his life by the tying together of his past with his present; the indispensible role of institutions for the acquisition of all man's skills, knowledge, self-understanding, stories, symbols, and sense of reality. And, of course, the critical role which culture plays in providing models, illuminating stories, organizing data, selecting goals, and serving as a specific guide to behavior for man's stories.[6]

Sam Keen, who is less institutionally and politically oriented than either Novak or Cox, is no longer
active as a theologian or academician in the traditional sense. Reared as a Southern Presbyterian, Keen took
a Ph.D. at Harvard and taught for some time at Louisville Presbyterian Theological Seminary. In 1970 Keen
left his academic post in Louisville, Kentucky, and
became a free-lance lecturer, writer, and group leader
in sensitivity training and group work-shops associated
both with the Center for the Study of Persons at La
Jolla, California, and with the well known Esalen Institute at Big Sur, California. At about the same time
he became a Consulting Editor to Psychology Today.
Keen refers to this period of his life as a particularly traumatic time when reaching the mythical age of
forty he left the security of seventeen years of marriage and got a divorce, dropped out of academic life,
relocated to California, and took up a new profession.[7]

The Loss of Wonder

In his book Apology For Wonder (1969) Keen makes
it clear that the autobiographical concern has played
a significant role in the way in which he has developed
the subject of "wonder." It was his quest for self-
understanding of the deep experiences of "wonder and
skepticism" that led him to a closer examination of the
phenomena of "wonder" and its critical role for authentic human existence.[8]

Keen insists that Western man's loss of the sense
of wonder, as well as his loss of the sense of the
"holy," of cosmic reason, and the notion of the "death
of God," and the phenomena of the "secularization" of
Western culture, are the results of the unsolved split
between the sacred and the profane. The concept of
this split has been bequeathed to Western culture by
the Judeo-Christian tradition.[9] This tradition has
fostered a kind of practical or functional dualism
by its stress upon the "Wholly Other God" — known
only through special revelation — and the secular or
profane world which, although filled with much which
is meaningful, is no longer a medium for God. Keen
cites three factors which have contributed to the
skepticism about the traditional Christian idea of God.
First, the impact which historical and literary crit-

icism has had upon Biblical texts has led many to a
serious questioning of the validity and uniqueness of
Biblical religion. Secondly, the rise of urban culture
has made man more aware of his religious pluralism,
of the multiple truth claims, and revelational claims
of many religions. And, finally, Keen contends that
there is a widespread shift in the spiritual loyalities
of contemporary man to the pragmatic and to controlling
that which is in the immediate environment.[10] Contemporary man is simply indifferent to the gods or the
God of former ages.

A major consequence of this prevailing mood has
been to foster the notion that "God" actually becomes
a barrier to man's freedom. Man is free to make himself what he will be only if he can be completely free
to create his own values. Therefore, man must banish
the holy, the sacred, even God, from his world in order
to become completely free. Secular man is on his own,
totally free and totally responsible. The world is
neutral, not working on his behalf — grace has been
banished. He is the product of chance. Man must now
form his self-identity in a void — in nothingness.[11]

This new condition of secular man calls for another
model of man which will lead him back to wholeness and
health, according to Keen. Such a model, Keen's ideal
man, is "homo tempestivus."[12] Homo tempestivus is
the man for all seasons. He knows when to act and how
to act. He maintains the delicate balance between a
sense of wonder and action. He is the healthy or mature
man. He recognizes and maintains the tension between
the Dionysian way (characterized by the impulsive dis-
regard for boundaries) and the Apollonian way (characterized by an orderly observation of the metaphysical,
social, and religious limits).[13] In short, Keen's
appeal is for a man who is neither suspicious of nor
resentful of the natural sensual nature of his being,
but a man who will place trust in his body and its
natural surroundings which nourish him and have confidence in his human impulses and enjoy the simplicity
and directness of experience. Keen would create a new
consciousness in Western man — one which would reunite
body and mind, self and world, wonder and action. Indeed, for Keen, from the religious perspective the
sacred must be incarnate in flesh, in events, and in
things or it is not incarnate at all.[14]

14

Keen pursues this theme of overcoming the alienating dualisms experienced by contemporary man further in his publication To A Dancing God. He is fond of quoting Arthur Darby Nock, a Harvard historian of religions, as saying that "Primitive religion is not believed. It is danced."[15] It is Keen's contention that there are certain metaphysical conceptions, and certain emotions, which are difficult to understand without motion or bodily movement. He notes that even Plato recognized the importance of gymnastics and the dance for political education, and that the dance was the chief way in which primitive societies celebrated and exhibited their beliefs and value systems.[16] But primitive man accepted his identity with nature, with his flesh, and he recognized his dependency upon the seasonal rhythm of nature. Therefore, he expressed his beliefs and his life story through the dance and other direct bodily rituals. He gave candid expression to his fears, his joys, his loves, and the experience of the ecstatic and mysterious with his body.

Overcoming Dualisms

Keen's thesis is that man will overcome the dualisms perpetuated in Western culture — whether they be of the spirit-flesh, mind-body, imagination-action, meaning-fact type or of the self-world, man-God type— if he can revive the "story" as a basic instrument for the "formation of identity." Indeed, Keen insists that the notion of "the death of God" is best understood as the expression of men who can no longer believe that the meaning of life can attain ultimate significance when it is incorporated into a story — such as the Judeo-Christian story. He suggests that storytelling is "functionally" the same as believing in God.[17]

Keen notes that primitive man lived in a world which attained its social, religious, and intellectual structure through storytelling. Each tribe had its own tales about its origins, the history of its social rituals, legends of its metaphysical role, and specific models or heroes who were to be emulated. A necessary part of tribal membership involved the retelling and the acting out of these shared legends, tales, and myths on a regular basis so that they would be perpetuated from generation to generation. In that context the story served the same functions as theology, philosophy, ethics, history, and drama do today. The story

located man within the cosmos, within nature, the community, and the family. But the story also created a
picture of precisely what was expected of man within
all of these contexts and what he, in turn, might ex-
pect beyond life after death. The story was the primary formative factor for both culture and self-identity.

Keen insists that traditional man found the affirmation of his integral relationship to the whole of
reality through the story. Storytelling gave man a
history, a present, and the possibilities of a future
within the context of meaningful relationships with
nature, community, family, and cosmos. It gave traditional man a sense of moral, spiritual, and physical
harmony with his universe. In telling his stories man
could have confidence that, despite his limited perspective and role in the scale of Being, he had found
the key to its unity.[18]

Recovery of the Holy

However, contemporary man, for numerous reasons,
has lost his confidence in the metaphysical and religious stories of tradition, according to Keen. So
what is man to do? Is he condemned to live in a world
ruled by chance where every man must give what little
meaning he can to his own existence? Can man recover
a meaningful sense of identity with continuity after
"the death of God?" Keen believes that man can rediscover a sense of identity and a vision of the holy if
he will start with his own story.

If there is any underlying principle which will
help a man recover a sense of the sacred, or the holy,
it must be found in that which is immediately experienced, touched, or felt by him. In operational terms,
says Keen, that which provides personal meaning, value,
dignity, depth, and unity to man qualifies as the
sacred or the holy and becomes the rightful domain of
theological investigation.[19] When man reflects upon
his own history he discovers that his autobiography is
(psychologically, socially, and biologically) the autobiography of every man.[20] The mixed hatred and love
of an Oedipus for his father is the psychological experience of every man when he reflects upon it. And
the rebellion against God is only a short step away
from the hating of the father. In the depths of each

16

man's personal story is the story of Adam or Pro-
metheus — the story of all the heroes and antiheroes
who have crossed the stage of history or frequented the
myths and legends of the past.

For Keen, any language is theological if it points
to that which is experienced as sacred or holy. With
this understanding of theological language, Keen proceeds to define the "holy" as that primal "principle,
power, or presence" which is the origin of and the
assurance of value, meaning, dignity, unity, and wholeness.[21] With this descriptive, functional definition
of the "holy" Keen insists that it is not located in
the supernatural somewhere but in the everyday, the
natural — carnal flesh itself! If God is no longer
recognized as the Transcendent One, he must be found
in the temporal realm. In place of a "unique incarnation" in history, the holy must be recognized in the
persons, principles, and powers presently at work to
maintain human dignity. If the incarnation means anything more than a mere historical event, declares Keen,
it must mean that healing, wholeness, grace comes
through the flesh.[22] When man recovers this sense of
the holy, he will realize his identity with the rest of
mankind (the collective story) and with the whole
cosmos (the metaphysical story — the story of the gods
or God). It is on this basis that Keen sketches the
outline of what he initially calls "Visceral Theology"
but which he later calls "Erotic Theology."[23]

Borrowing a line from Merleau-Ponty (the Phenomenologist and Gestalt psychologist, see Chapter Five on
Phenomenological Theology), Keen insists that man's
point of entry into nature, or his "bridge" to life,
is the body. The body, therefore, becomes man's
"model" by which he experiences and learns to understand and trust his entire cosmos. The attitude which
a man develops about his own body will be the attitude
which he holds about the rest of his world. There
exists a high correlation between the way a man feels
about his body and the attitude he holds about the
social-political order, nature, and his metaphysical
vision. If a man can experience the grace of his carnality, he can experience the grace, the trustworthi-
ness, the succor, the strength of nature and the sacredness of life.[24]

While "visceral theology" starts with carnal man and insists that all knowledge is limited to the scope of historical experience, it recognizes that man's "horizon" of life is not so limited and that there is an undeniable mystery which surrounds each human existence. Keen compares these known and unknown elements of man's identity to the Gestalt notion of the figure-ground. To understand man he must be seen against a cosmic background.

Keen believes that Christianity and Christian theology has functioned very much in the same manner as ancient Gnosticism by promoting many of the dualisms which have distorted contemporary Western man's appreciation for the wholeness of life. For instance, since the time of the Protestant Reformation the stress on the "hearing" of the Word of God by the ear of faith has further perpetuated this fragmentation of life. Visceral theology, he asserts, places the stress on "touching" rather than just hearing. Man must rediscover the sacred in that which moves him, touches him, makes him tremble, in that which is ordinary rather than something extra-ordinary, that which is immediate rather than distant or remote. Visceral theology, or Erotic Theology, is not separated from nature, sexuality, and carnality. It engages in the resensitizing and re-educating of man in the sacredness which lies hidden in his very visceral. The time when concepts, doctrines, words, and abstract ideas touch and move men is past, declares Keen. While words and ideas have their place in the religious experience of the sacred, that which is called for now is the word which can be felt in the flesh — the dance.[25]

Keen uses Rudolf Otto's classical phenomeno-logical description of the holy — as the __mysterium: tremendum et fascinans__[26] — (that mystery which is at once both awesome - frightening - tremendous, or Totally Other, and fascinating - desirable - compelling for man) as a basis for pointing up the mystery which man experiences in his own body. The "mystery of God" which man experiences in his body is not something which can be located at this point or that point but refers to the human capacity to experience freedom, grace, or that nothingness — the Void. For Keen there is no "mystery of God" unless man also experiences a void, or emptiness. And that which makes man tremble is most frequently experienced in sexuality. And the

18

idea of the desirable, the compelling, the fascinating is experienced in the throes of pain, pleasure, love, and loneliness.[27]

The kind of theology which contemporary man needs, according to Keen, is not so much a theology of the head as a theology of the flesh. A theology that will heal the split of centuries of dualistic thinking and resurrect the sacredness of the human body whose feelings and desires will restore man to a sense of oneness, or wholeness, with his brothers and with nature. The kind of theology which will place more emphasis upon the exploration of man's interior world of feeling and emotions and less emphasis upon investigating the exterior world of religions, doctrines, ideas, and things.

COX

While Keen's storytelling theology ends up placing him in a rather radical sensitivity-encounter or human-potential movement camp, Harvey Cox avoids this extreme and endeavors to take a much broader perspective for his theological stance. Indeed, this point is well illustrated by his assessment of the sensitivity-encounter or human-potential movement which he writes about in The Seduction of the Spirit. In a cleverly entitled chapter "Naked Revival: Theology and the Human Potential Movement" Cox recounts the story of his own experiences with the sensitivity-encounter movement at the Esalen Institute in Big Sur, California. While admitting that his experiences there constituted a critical turning point for him, in terms of returning to a trust in his own emotions and feelings and recognizing the importance of this element for religion, Cox goes on to give a social-political, religious-cultural analysis.[28] His experience in the hot sulfer baths, for example, cause him to reflect upon the unique function which "clothes" have in society to symbolize status, power, liberation, and the threat of punishment to people. This brings him to certain comments about the place of liturgical vestments if the Christian Community is really concerned about the priesthood of believers.

Of greater importance, however, is the significance which Cox perceives in the touching and bodily expressions of concern and warmth encouraged by the movement for Christian worship. Jesus regularly touch-

19

ed people and the New Testament contains frequent references to the disciples "laying on of hands" and the "Kiss of Peace." And in John 13, Jesus specifically directs his followers to wash each others feet. Cox is convinced that bodily gestures should be an integral part of the religious life, a fact which he observes is characteristic of South American Christianity in which dancing and much hugging, embracing, and physical gesturing is commonplace. However, this concern, about what he calls the "new pietism," is not merely the susceptibility toward abuses of exploitation and promiscuity or emotional fanaticism. Cox's concern with sensory-awareness tendencies in today's culture is the peril which such may hold for political and social activism and relevance. He fears that the new pietism may lead either to massive retreat from political involvement or to a completely internalized, subjective ethic.[29]

Perhaps a part of the acute concern which Harvey Cox has for political and social involvement can be traced back to his early years in Malvern, Pennsylvania, where he was born in 1929. In his autobiographical account of the first seventeen years of his life in that "Tribal Village" Cox describes it as the town which everything and everyone seemed to bypass — from the Pennsylvania Railroad, the highway, and industry to Presidential candidates.[30]

Cox received his undergraduate education at the University of Pennsylvania and took a B.D. degree at Yale Divinity School, Yale University in 1955. From 1955 to 1958 he served as Director of Religious Activities at Oberlin College, Oberlin, Ohio, before going on to Harvard University for a Ph.D. degree. An ordained minister in the American Baptist Church, Cox, through an arrangement made with the World Council of Churches, spent the year 1962-63 as an ecumenical fraternal worker in East Berlin involved in adult education. He returned to the United States in the Fall of 1963 as Assistant Professor of Theology and Culture at Andover Newton Theological School where he taught for the next two years. With the publication of The Secular City and his appointment to Harvard Divinity School, as Associate Professor of Church and Society, in 1965, Cox's charm and popularity as a critic of religions and cultural traditions spread rapidly. This reputation was further advanced and given a greater ecumenical thrust with the publication of another best seller The Feast of Fools (1969).

When Harvey Cox wrote The Secular City he had just returned from Berlin, Germany, where he had spent the better part of his year thinking about the implications of Dietrich Bonhoeffer's notions of "religionless Christian," a "religionless world," and a world "come of age" since God had been "edged out of the world."[31] It had also been a year during which Cox had been engaged in dialogue with East German Marxist concerning the relevance of Christianity in today's world. Reacting to the tremendous impact which this year abroad had had upon his thinking Cox endeavored to do for the American scene what he felt Bonhoeffer had done for the European scene. Consequently, The Secular City was his declaration that the modern urban-secular man was not mourning the loss of the religious world-view, rather he was celebrating his new found freedom in the functional development of urban technology. The relativization of values, the conscious awareness of pluralistic religious and philosophical viewpoints, were all a part of the secularization process which urban-man in the anonymity and mobility of "technopolis" recognized as a liberating process. Clearly the task of those who live by the biblical faith was to "nourish" this process and make certain that it did not develop into a new dogmatic world-view ("secularism").[32]

At that time in history, Cox believed that what was demanded of Christians in order to speak meaningfully to secular man was a revolutionary theology of political or social action which would meet head-on the rapid social changes of the secular city. Such a theology would be characterized by "maturity" and "responsibility" since secularization itself was understood as a process of maturing and, therefore, the process of assuming more and more self-responsibility. Secularization symbolized that man's metaphysical and religious supports had been removed and that he was now completely on his own. Hence, for Cox, the "modern equivalent of repentance" was to use social and political power responsibly.[33]

A Larger Concept of Religion

While Cox admits that "the city" has always represented something very positive for him, and that The Secular City was in essence his salute to the satis-

21

fying liberation which the anonymity of the city gave him, it is obvious that when he wrote The Feast of Fools five years later that his thinking had undergone some changes. Perhaps the most notable point of change has to do with the value and place of "religion" in general for the life of man. Influenced by Bonhoeffer, Cox asserted in The Secular City that urban-secular man was not bemoaning the loss of a religious world-view because the world had always appeared "devoid" of any cosmic meaning for him.[34] Whereas in The Feast of Fools, the primary focus of which is upon "festivity" and "fantasy," religion has been restored to an absolutely essential role in the life of man if he is to rise above a mundane, empirical existence.[35] This recognition of a broad religious sensibility (that which Tillich called man's "ultimate concern" and which he believed was characteristic of man) is even further affirmed by Cox in his most recent book — The Seduction of The Spirit. In this latter work "religion" has been defined in a very broad way to include all those components in an individual's or a group's life which pull it together and bind it into a "meaningful whole."[36]

Theology of the Clown

Cox confesses that whereas in The Secular City he was a little too "Protestant," even Puritan, with his stress on activism, social change, and responsibility, in The Feast of Fools he is much more Dionysian. He asserts that something of the playful, jubilant, festive, sensuous, joyous spirit is forcefully returning to Christianity and that he believes a "rebirth of festivity" will lead Christians through the "crisis" called the death of God.[37] True to form as the avant-garde theologian, Cox assesses the religious pulse of 1969 as having moved beyond the deification of the present (the "Radical Theology" of the death of God movement as represented by Thomas Altizer, William Hamilton, and Richard Rubenstein)[38] and as recognizing the inadequacy of almost identifying God completely with the future (what is basically a European theological emphasis of Jürgen Moltmann and Johannes Metz — the "Theology of Hope").[39] He asserts that the correct "mood" of the times, in terms of religious sensibility, is one of "comic hope" and this calls for a theology of contrast, creative discontinuity, a kind of theological clownishness which Cox labels as a "Theology of Juxtaposition."[40]

A Theology of Juxtaposition will do one important thing, which religion has always done, which is to link together man's past with the present (which Radical Theology virtually negated by its extreme focus upon the "present crisis" of faith), and still not deny the importance of the future (the overemphasis found in the Theology of Hope) for faith. It will help man maintain the tensions of these three dimensions of temporality precisely by focusing upon those points where memory, experience, and hope challenge and contradict each other. Those points of challenge and contradiction for Cox are "festivity" and "fantasy." He insists that both are essential for the survival and vitality of man.

In festivity man takes a brief interlude from his ordinary routine in life to celebrate, or affirm, some event, or occasion in such a way that it contrasts with everyday life by its excessiveness.[41] Festivity, therefore, necessitates some focus upon history, the past, or memory, some special time or occasion to be remembered or anticipated. It helps man stay alive to time by relating the three dimensions of time to each other. Fantasy, according to Cox, is letting the imagination "soar" with no holds barred. It allows for conscious creativity and has an artistic element in it. Much like the stuff of which dreams are made it can become perilous when it loses its connection to fact and reason. But fantasy demands hope, it is more concerned with the future dimension. Cox compares it theologically to the image of God in man — it allows man to create entire worlds out of nothing.[42]

Juxtaposition theology, like the clown or the jester, challenges the seriousness of tradition and the past by mocking displays while simultaneously incorporating that tradition into man's present experience (the festival). But at the same time, juxtaposition theology limits the excessive claims of both the past and the present by its expressions of hope for the future (fantasy). According to The Feast of Fools, what Christians need to do is reappropriate some of the radical impulses of their tradition, such as monasticism, sectarianism, and utopianism, and rediscover some of the life styles of early Christians and some of the images of the Christ which have virtually been forgotten. Some of these radical life styles have begun to reappear, according to Cox, in communes and co-

23

ops; but his nomination for the image of Christ which today's world needs is seldom seen — that of the "Harlequin" (the clown).

In an age that has almost completely lost its appreciation for fantasy and the traditions of the festival, particularly the religious festival, the clown personifies both. It is the clown who despite his being constantly humiliated, beaten down, and defeated always comes back. By clothing Christ as a clown Cox contends that Christians express their personal and collective experiences of doubt and disillusionment, as well as the irony and depth of their hope. "Christ the clown signifies our playful appreciation of the past and our comic refusal to accept the spectre of inevitability in the future. He is the incarnation of festivity and fantasy."[43]

Expanding the Theme

In The Seduction of the Spirit Cox expands upon the theological notion of "juxtaposition" while incorporating a much broader base for the substance of his religious concerns. While expressing real doubts about the future of theology, he is much more certain about the future of the "human spirit" of which theology is only one form of its religious expression. In fact, Cox declares that theology is a "reflective, analytical, objective" form of thought which has arisen only in "recent centuries" (a remark which would arouse considerable surprise, if not debate, in most theological circles).[44] He then proceeds to outline three aspects of a future theology as a kind of "play" or "harlequinesque theology."

What theologians should be doing in the future, as Cox sees it, can be described, first of all, as "making fun of," debunking, satirizing, or lampooning all symbols, myths, values, institutions, and sacred texts which are destructive of human liberation. An integral part of the theologian's task is to play the role of the "holy fool," the clown, the jester wherever religious or political leaders would promote pretentious and spurious claims.[45] Secondly, theologians should be involved in imaginative transformation of symbols and fantasizing about new and unlikely images of God, man, and the world. They should be comparing improbable concepts, exploring possible metaphors, "making believe" they are someone else — a Sioux brave, a sixteenth-

24

century Carmelite nun, or a Zen Master. Theology as
"make believe" should be exploring the possibilities of
experiencing the interior feelings and alternative consciousness of other religious traditions and faith
positions.[46]

The experiencing of other religious views has become a very important part of Cox's theological approach today. Indeed, it appears to be critical for
what he considers as an apologetic form of theology.
He contends that while many people feel estranged from
their own religious traditions they are intrigued by
some of the more unusual imported religions, but are
unable to experience them to any satisfying degree. At
the same time there are those who feel no identity with
the religious experience whatsoever. Neither group,
according to Cox, would be the least interested in a
brilliant, persuasive, intellectual theological defense
of religion — a new theological synthesis (or <u>Summa</u>
<u>Theologica</u>). However, they might be enticed to get in-
volved if someone could lead them into a meaningful
experience. Therefore, the number one task of theologians today is to learn from the gurus and shamans,
what they have mastered, the art of helping people experience and encounter the vast reality of the universe
which is now missing from their lives. Cox is convinced that the theology of the future must begin with
experience, testimony, and confessions and then move
on to its more formal, traditional, functions.[47] The
only point at which theologians might begin to learn
such a feeling and consciousness for these other religious traditions is with the almost forgotten childhood
experience of "making believe" they are someone else.

The third way in which theology can become "play"
challenges the current cultural prejudice which decrees
that everything be useful, productive, or instrumental.
Theology, like play, is a "useless" activity which
serves no purpose beyond itself in a society that is
designed for production, efficiency and showing results. Cox asserts that, paradoxically, theology has a
kind of summons for man to decide about his future —
"an eschatological word" — in a culture which is
tempted to let technology rule. Indeed, it may offer
the only alternative images of the future for modern
man. Theology should remind man that productive work
is not all there is to life and, in this sense, should
always be a little "useless."[48]

25

The Seduction of The Spirit is actually an illustration of theology as a "playful" activity. But it is also a monument to Cox's expanded consciousness and recognition of the primal importance of "religion" in the lives of men in general. At one point Cox admits that the book is in part a "defense" of the great "variety" of religious expressions of mankind, as well as an apology for the "reality of religion" in opposition to those skeptics who dismiss it for one reason or another.[49]

As indicated earlier, Cox defines "religion" as that cluster of elements — rites, customs, myths, hopes, images and memories — which pull together the life of an individual or a group into a meaningful whole. He contends that in most cultures religion is an integrated part of the whole society and that it has only been in modern Western culture that religion has been restricted to an association with mosques, synagogues and churches.[50] This fact is most evident, according to Cox, when the themes of mass media, people's religion, and autobiography are examined (the major themes of The Seduction of The Spirit).

Storytelling

Following the lead of his theological colleagues (Novak and Keen) Cox discusses the primal human act of storytelling as being of two kinds. First, the personal, autobiographical story, which Cox likes to designate as "testimony" and which the contemplatives or mystics of an earlier era called "interiority."[51] And, secondly, the collective story, which Cox calls "People's Religion." People's Religion is a kind of corporate testimony which embraces the identity, dignity and survival instincts of a human group. It includes a groups' fantasies, superstitions, customs, memories (nostalgias) and hopes. It is the unsophisticated folk religion which finds expression both within and outside formal ecclesiastical institutions. It includes both current "pop" type and preliterate or "primitive" type rituals and liturgies. It gives expression to the real "soul" of a people; especially, the poor, the oppressed, the losers, the victims, the hurt, the captives, and if it dies the people die. For Cox the best example of "Peoples' Religion" is to be seen in the black Christianity of America.

The black slaves prevented their own extinction and absorption into the white culture in part by creatively adopting the distorted Christianity which was forced upon them into their own ancestral religion. In this respect, people's religion is not only a survival technique but it may also become an important link with preliterate religions which Cox contends is well illustrated in Latin American Mariology piety with its Our Lady of Guadalupe adaptation.[52]

There is a third type of religion, besides testimony and people's religion, which Cox designates as "signals." "Signals" in contrast to storytelling is a less human form of communication (animals use signals almost exclusively — the chirp of a bird, the howl or bark of a dog). People are storytellers. However, whereas stories serve to bind people together emotionally, historically and in terms of values, signals make possible much more complex types of human unification through codification and systematization. Signal religion is the kind of religion which is controlled and propagated by specialists, such as clerics. Nearly all the major religions of mankind are a mixture of storytelling and signal religion. Signal religion is Cox's way of indicating what is essentially institutionalized religion. Its emphasis is upon systems, reason, clarity and specificity.[53]

Cox argues that religion should be the source of new stories for people but that today it is not fulfilling this primal role of storytelling. Rather, he contends that like the rest of society it is overburdened with systems and signals. Therefore, he insists, the time has come for a "rebirth" of both testimony and people's religion.

There are three traditional functions which have always been identifiable in religion which holds true for both the storytelling type or the signal type. There is, first of all, an attempt on the part of religion to explain man's origin, where he came from and how he got to be the way he is. Secondly, religion always points man in the direction he must go if he is to become "saved," or made whole, or fulfill his destiny. It elevates some "ideal possibility" for man. Finally, religion always shows man how to overcome his lost, sick, or fallen condition. It shows him the way of "grace."

Disguised Religion

On the basis of these three traditional functions
of religion, Cox contends that there is another type
of "signal" religion in society today which is an even
greater threat to storytelling religion than are the
huge organized churches. It is the religion which the
culture theologian identifies as the "mass media." It
is a particularly insidious form of signal religion because it is not recognized by most people as being a
religion at all. However, Cox points out how it fulfills all the traditional functions of religion. Television shows and popular magazine ads are full of myths
and heroes. They supply the viewer or reader with
models for making decisions, checking out his percep-
tions, and finding a life style. The mass media has
its priests who proclaim that man's great transgressions
are his foul breath, wet armpits, or dull hair, and that
the real saints are all using this mouth wash, or that
deodorant, and are the models of free, competent, attractive human beings. But the "good news" is that
this life of freedom, competence, and attractiveness is
available to all for the asking (and a certain amount
of cash in hand). Cox insists that the religion of
mass media seldom lets man out of its temple. That it
enjoys much more power and influence in determinig life
style and value systems than most critics are willing
to admit, and that it should be recognized for what it
is — a disguised religion.[54]

Having argued for a proper balance between stories
and signals in religion, and warning that in today's
society there is an overloading of signals, Cox proceeds to alert people to an additional distortion which
has arisen between story and signal. It is the mis-
representation which occurs when signals try to "pose"
as stories. Cox calls this procedure the "seduction of
the spirit."[55] It is a calculated exploitation or
twisting of people's natural, healthy religious instincts. Its purpose is to deceive and mislead for
the purposes of controlling, manipulating, and dominat-
ing people. The seducer is really a "signaler" pre-
tending to be a storyteller. Cox insists that it is
the most ruthless assault on religion because it en-
tices a man to become a party to his own self-deception.

In the light of his expanded interpretation of religion, Cox believes that Western culture is witnessing an impressive "rebirth of spiritual energy" today which ranges across a broad spectrum of expressions including everything from outbursts of healing services in Episcopal churches to Hare Krishna dancers chanting on street corners in major cities.[56] He is convinced that the primary direction of this spiritual renewal (or "revival of piety") lies in the quest for inwardness, or the recovery of the "soul" through meditation, contemplation, or "interiority" (testimony). The direction of this quest is given added incentive by the tendencies of organized religious groups which, being confused by this unexpected spiritual outburst, give even more momentum to their signal-heavy organizations. The perplexity of the situation will become lessened when the churches realize that the real conflict is not between emotion and reason, or faith and reason, or even science and religion. But that the true source of contention is more easily understood as the rebellion of man, the storyteller and symbol maker, against a culture which has gone too far in the use of cues and signals.

Religion's Proper Role

Therefore, as Cox sees it, the proper role for religion to play in a "healthy culture" would be that of maintaining the balance between storytelling and signals, heart and head, mystics and priests, visionaries and systematizers. But religion in the present sick culture of the West must side with the underdog. It must restore its own health, as well as that of the culture, if necessary by sacrificing its structure to spirit, its form to renewed piety, its signals to stories, its systems to people's religion. Like the theologian — a la Harvey Cox — the churches, the top-heavy religious signalers of the present day, must play the role of the clown, the critic, the corrective and renounce the ways of the seducer.

The primal act of "testimony," man telling his story, must be restored not only to theology but to signal religion as well.[57] Theology, in its clownish, playful, "make believe" role must make an informed, critical, sympathetic response to religion in its broadest most inclusive form — "People's Religion." Its criterion for proceeding must be no less than that of the emancipation of the people from political and

29

economic bondage (symbolized by the Exodus) and liberation (symbolized by Easter) from whatever enslaves them
to the past ("sin") or frightens them about the future
("death").[58] Theology pursued under the norm of liberation, which Cox understands as a mere enlargement of
the theme of emancipation, will reveal the false myths
and seductive procedures of the powerful and bring about
a radical form of consciousness (or "faith") that will
continuously reshape the meaning of reality.[59].

The two procedures which Cox advocates for doing
theology under the liberation criterion are those
which help him to understand what religion really means
for people involved in it today. The first approach
combines some of the elements of traditional textual
interpretation (hermeneutics) with a method used by the
social scientist ("participant observer") which Cox
designates as "participant hermeneutics."[60] This
approach endeavors to maximize an understanding of
both the ideological background and context of people's
religion as well as the objective-observer-participant
role. It demands that the theologian be responsive and
not merely descriptive. The second approach incorporates a theological appreciation for the tradition and
structure of religious ritual with an experimental or
trial method. Cox calls it "experimental liturgics."[61]
The assumption behind it seems to be that there are
stories, symbols, and rituals within a religious tradition that can find new meaning and still have a powerful affect upon people if restructured by the people
themselves and placed in another setting, environment
or time span which is more subject to contemporary expression.

The theologian who accepts the norm of human
liberation and sets himself to the task of understanding and supporting people's religion must, says Cox,
learn to move back and forth between the poles of particularity and the universal.[62] The theologian whose
particular religious consciousness is nurtured by
Christianity needs to understand the variegated religious expressions of human liberation as found among
Hindus, Buddists, and "Third World" religions if he
is to be shaken from his own provincialism on the subject. At the same time, the theologian who endeavors
to hold only a universal religious consciousness finds
himself floundering around in a kind of "global re-
ligiousity." The tension must be maintained if genuine

human liberation is to be served. For Cox, the kind of religious and political life that would best serve the needs of human liberation must be focused primarily at the two ends of the continuum — the local and the global. The religious and political organizations (or politics) of the future must do away with National states and denominational loyalties. People's loyalties must focus upon global humankind and the local community in which they are most realistically immersed. The religious consciousness most needed today is one that is intensely local and inclusively global.[63]

Having attained his theological prominence primarily by a theology of culture, Cox believes that theologians must at the present time provide a critical assessment of the mass media. This he asserts is especially important since the mass media is functioning as a disguised religion, by propagating value patterns and doing it in the most seductive manner. Following the central thesis of the late Paul Tillich that the responsibility of a theology of culture is to point to the religious dimension of man's cultural life, and, therefore, nothing lies outside the theologian's scope of concern, Cox serves notice that there are three points at which his approach to culture differs from that of Tillich.[64] First, his focus is much more upon the visual images — TV, films, magazine ads, etc. — than the verbal images or symbols. Second, he is more interested in the popular cultural expressions — cinema, comics, photography, technical design, etc. — than with the classic creations. Third, Cox is more concerned about what he calls the "dynamics" of culture, especially, "revolutionary" elements — the political and social interaction of groups and forces within the culture — than Tillich seemed to be.

Cox draws upon the experience of Eastern Orthodoxy in his endeavor to demonstrate the value which the visual image (the icon) has for religious practice. His contention is that until recently the "icon" has implied an object for visual contemplation and the "machine" has been considered an object for manipulation. Now, however, since the advent of TV, film, and modern advertising, this separation can no longer be maintained. Modern technology has become not merely instrumental but, also, contemplative. Photography and television are both instruments of contemplation and manipulation. Cox insists that the theologian must steer a course between the anti-media critics and the mass media buffs in recognizing the values and possibilities of the new icon.[65] In theory he insists that television, film, and other types of news media have tremendous possibilities for communicating greater understanding, equality, and spiritual community. Under different controls the electronic media could be the major means of attaining a "global village."

Under present one-way communication devices, which dominate the mass media technology, dialogue is prevented. Cox believes that the particularity of his Christian tradition supplies him with a set of stories, values, and images which give him a vantage point for evaluating and judging the present mass media message. The essential character of Jesus' life and ministry illustrates that real communication takes place in community. Men cannot give their testimonies, tell their stories, or participate in the development of their own liberties, when encouraged to be mere consumers, viewers, and listeners. The theologian, and the churches, must as advocates of human liberation realize that man cannot live without a story. The mass media, however, is supplying man with a story today that will keep him weak and vulnerable unless a theology of mass communications exposes its falseness (especially to the peoples of the underdeveloped countries and the weak, and poor, and powerless of the world), and promotes a mass media based upon the facilitation of dialogue and community.[66] For Cox decentralization should be the goal not only for governments and giant religious organizations, but for the electronic media as well.

What can be said for the approach of the cultural or story theologians of today? Certainly the Christian faith must, if it is to survive, speak meaningfully, critically, and constructively (when possible) of the cultural milieu. To the extent that story theology makes contemporary man more aware of his own identity and responsibility, it fulfills a rightful function of Christian theology and religion in general. Man needs to tell his personal story. There is a time and a place for "testimony." Individually and collectively man has an insatiable curiosity about his origin, purpose, and destiny. But does "people's religion," or the collective story, really satisfy man's desire for a meaningful faith experience? How helpful is a theology which has assumed such a broad definition of religion that it virtually embraces the whole of culture? When religion is defined as whatever it is in culture that draws together the life of the individual or the group into a significant whole, has not the uniqueness of religion already been sacrificed to any number of cultural phenomena? And when the theologian resorts to body sensations and interiority as the substance of his theological critique, has he not already given up his role as theologian?

FOOTNOTES

[1]For further commentary on this tendency in theology see the article by Carl Raschke, "The Fantasies of the New Theologians," The Christian Century, May 15, 1974, pp. 533-37. However, in contrast to this popular approach or tendency, there is an emerging group of Biblical scholars who are very much interested in developing a systematic hermeneutic of the parabolic narratives of the Old and New Testaments. See, for example, "A Symposium on Story and Narrative in Theology," in Theology Today, Vol. XXXII (July, 1975). Note especially the articles by George W. Stroup, III, "A Bibliographical Critique," pp. 133-143, and Sallie McFague TeSelle, "The Experience of Coming to Belief," pp. 159-165. Dr. TeSelle's new book, Speaking in Parables: A Study in Metaphor and Theology (Fortress Press, 1975), is an expansion of the thesis set forth in the brief article published in Theology Today.

[2]Cf. his book, The Feast of Fools (Harvard University Press, 1969), pp. 165-177, for intellectual and theological currents which have become normative for his doing of theology.

[3]Vietnam: Crisis of Conscience was authored by R. M. Brown, Abraham J. Heschel, and Novak (a Protestant, a Jew, and a Catholic and published by their respective presses — Association Press, Behrman House, Herder and Herder) to spark the interfaith community into open opposition to the war in Vietnam. In A Theology For Radical Politics (Herder and Herder, 1969), Novak called attention to the concerns of the "New Left" for a revolutionary employment of power, a new sense of community, and the demand for authenticity in human relations (p. 17). He noted then that a revolution in the human consciousness was taking place in America and the Western world and that the task of Christians, if they were to salvage any of the younger generation of leaders for the future, was to become more human and less Christian, more open to nature, to the experience of community, to sexual love, to faith in man, and honesty, and less concerned about parochial dogmas and tradition (Cf. chapters 6 and 7.

[4]See Ascent of the Mountain, Flight of the Dove (Harper & Row, 1971), pp. xi-xvi; also, Michael Novak,, "The Identity Crisis of Us All: Response to Professor Crouter," Journal of The American Academy of Religion, XL (March, 1972), 66, 73.

[5] See _Ascent of the Mountain, Flight of the Dove_, pp. 67, 68; 45.

[6] Cf. _ibid._, pp. 26-27; 28, 41; 45, 60; 92-109; 120 _et passim_.

[7] See Sam Keen, _Voice and Visions_ (Harper & Row, 1974), pp. 4-5.

[8] Cf. his _Apology For Wonder_ (Harper & Row, 1969), pp. 14-17.

[9] See _ibid._, pp. 87-90.

[10] See _ibid._, pp. 108-110.

[11] Cf. _ibid._, pp. 110-114.

[12] See _ibid._, pp. 190-199.

[13] See _ibid._, p. 196.

[14] See _ibid._, p. 210.

[15] _To A Dancing God_ (Harper & Row, 1970), pp. 51; 160. Keen does not indicate precisely where Nock makes this statement.

[16] See _ibid._, pp. 51-52.

[17] See _ibid._, pp. 85-86.

[18] See _ibid._, pp. 87-99.

[19] See _ibid._, pp. 99ff.

[20] Cf. _ibid._, pp. 102-3. See also, _Voices and Visions_, p. 11, for another expression of his conviction that every man is impregnated with "archetypal" patterns.

[21] See _ibid._, p. 103; also, 157.

[22] See _ibid._, pp. 104-105; 144.

[23] In _To A Dancing God_ Keen's final chapter is entitled "The Importance of Being Carnal — Notes for a Visceral Theology," whereas in a paper written more recently and included in a book edited by John Y. Fenton, _Theology and Body_ (Westminster Press, 1974), Keen entitles his address "Toward An Erotic Theology," pp. 13-29. This paper gives a little sharper clarification of his most recent understanding of theology but does not essentially contradict what he outlined and gave expression to in _To A Dancing God_.

[24] See _To A Dancing God_, especially, the two principles or propositions, pp. 148, 155, _et passim_, Chapter Five.

[25] See _ibid._, pp. 159-160. Cf. his comments in "Toward An Erotic Theology," _op. cit._, p. 23, on the fact that in Eastern thought, which has had a religious impact upon Western man very recently, there has never been this notion that the head, or ideas, can triumphantly rule over the body of man. It has always recognized the importance of the visceral.

[26]See Rudolf Otto, The Idea of the Holy (Oxford University Press, 1958), Chapters IV, V, and VI. This book was first published in 1923.

[27]See "Toward An Erotic Theology," op. cit., pp. 27-29.

[28]See The Seduction of The Spirit: The Use and Misuse of People's Religion (Simon and Schuster, 1973), Chapter Eight.

[29]Cf. ibid., pp. 220-225.

[30]See ibid., pp. 23-26.

[31]See Bonhoeffer, Letters and Papers From Prison, edited by Eberhard Bethge (Revised Edition; The Macmillan Company, 1967), pp. 139-205, especially for his statements referred to in the text. See, also, Cox, The Seduction of The Spirit, pp. 123-131.

[32]Cf. The Secular City: Secularization and Urbanization in Theological Perspective (The Macmillan Company, 1965), especially, pp. 1-6; 18, 80; 82; 86; 36; et passim.

[33]Cf. ibid., Chapter 5, especially, pp. 107, 109, 119, 121; 254-268.

[34]See ibid., p. 80.

[35]See The Feast of Fools, pp. 68-69, 168, 173; cf., also, pp. 59, 43, 44, 125, et passim.

[36]See the whole Preface: "Religion as Story and Signal," pp. 9-19, but especially his definition on page 14.

[37]Cf. The Feast of Fools, pp. vii, 43, 55, et passim.

[38]See ibid., pp. 121-126.

[39]See ibid., pp. 126-130.

[40]See ibid., chapters 9 and 10.

[41]Cf. ibid., pp. 22-26; See pp. 7-18, for a general introduction to both festivity and fantasy.

[42]See ibid., chapter 4.

[43]Ibid., p. 142.

[44]See The Seduction of The Spirit, p. 319.

[45]Cf. ibid., pp. 319-320.

[46]Cf. ibid., pp. 320-325.

[47]See ibid., p. 324.

[48]Cf. ibid., pp. 325-329. Cox discussed "theologies of play and theologies of revolution" earlier in this book and indicates some of his sources and why he believes "play" informs his understanding of religion. See ibid., pp. 184-189.

[49]See *ibid.*, p. 318. See his discussion on "People's Religion," *ibid.*, Chapter four, especially his statement about how his attitude has changed regarding religion and its importance for marginalized peoples. pp. 121-122.

[50]See *ibid.*, p. 13.

[51]See *ibid.*, p. 9; chapter three, especially, p. 93.

[52]See *ibid.*, p. 10, chapter four, especially, pp. 117-119; chapter six, especially, p. 167, chapter seven, especially, pp. 176-180, 191-192.

[53]See *ibid.*, pp. 10-12; 106-107.

[54]Cf. *ibid.*, pp. 14-15.

[55]See *ibid.*, p. 16.

[56]See *ibid.*, pp. 17; 94-95.

[57]See *ibid.*, pp. 17-18; 96-97; 107-109; 112; 49-50.

[58]See *ibid.*, pp. 150-154.

[59]See *ibid.*, pp. 184-196.

[60]See *ibid.*, pp. 146-150.

[61]See *ibid.*, pp. 155-167. See his account of a "Byzantine Easter," pp. 156-160.

[62]See *ibid.*, pp. 152-155.

[63]See *ibid.*, Chapter Nine, especially, pp. 243, 251-257.

[64]See *ibid.*, pp. 263-267.

[65]See *ibid.*, Chapter Ten, especially, pp. 269-279.

[66]See *ibid.*, Chapter Twelve, especially, pp. 303-305, 307, 309-311, 313.

CHAPTER TWO

Liberation Theology

During the last half-dozen years there has been an increasing clamor on the part of many people in the Western hemisphere not only for a greater share in the distribution of the wealth and power of the developed nations, but, also, a greater demand for participation in the political and social decisions that affect the human destiny. It is only logical that theologians would find an apologetic role that would further these humanizing concerns during these times of great unrest and increasing awareness of the gross inequalities which exist within the human families of the world. This is precisely what has happened with a number of theologians whose theologies are here designated as "liberation theology." To ask what a black theologian in West Harlem, a Catholic Priest in Peru, and a female professor in New Haven, Connecticut, have in common is to ask the question "What does it mean to be fully human?" It is, also, to ask "What is the 'theology of liberation' all about?"

The theology of liberation soberly invites people to discover and realize the forms of common life which would destroy the dehumanizing tendencies of the present age. These dehumanizing tendencies are not something peculiar or unique to this period of human history but, rather, have reached such an intense level of consciousness that they can no longer be ignored or set aside as unimportant by serious Christians. An indication of this concern for human liberation can be recognized by this list of a few of the more recent books which deal with the subject: Rubem Alves, A Theology of Human Hope (1969); James Cone, A Black Theology of Liberation (1970); Gustavo Gutierrez, A Theology of Liberation (1972); Frederick Herzog, Liberation Theology (1972); J. Deotis Roberts, Liberation and Reconciliation: A Black Theology (1971); Rosemary Radford Ruether, Liberation Theology (1973); Letty M. Russell, Ferment of Freedom (1972), and Human Liberation in a Feminist Perspective - A Theology (1974); Mary Daly, Beyond God the Father: Toward a Philosophy of Women's Liberation (1973); William R. Jones, Is God a White Racist? A Preamble to Black Theology (1973); the proceedings of the 1974 convention of the College

Theology Society, edited by Thomas M. McFadden, Liberation, Revolution, and Freedom: Theological Perspectives (1975); and most recently a book written by a Vice President of the World Council of Churches Jose Miguez Bonino, Christians and Marxists: The Mutual Challenge to Revolution (1976).

The person who has done the most to identify the various aspects, concerns and sources of liberation theology and whose writings have treated the entire subject most systematically has been Letty M. Russell. Her most recent book Human Liberation in a Feminist Perspective - A Theology[1] is a significant contribution to theology and an unsurpassed guide for the student of liberation theology in general. In this work Russell has not only identified the common methods, themes, and perspectives of liberation theology and its major contributors, but she has personally demonstrated the development of such a theology.

Although Letty Russell is a rather recent arrival on the theological scene, she brings with her a wealth of practical experience working with the under-privileged, the Puerto Ricans, and the blacks in East Harlem, New York. An ordained minister in the United Presbyterian Church, Russell served as pastor in the East Harlem Protestant Parish from 1958-68. A long-time active participant in Christian women's movements and civil rights struggles, she is eminently qualified to express the feminist perspective on human liberation and its Christian implications. A 1951 graduate of Wellesley College, Russell received her S.T.B. at Harvard Divinity School in 1958, and an S.T.M., 1967, and Th.D., 1969, from Union Theological Seminary in New York. She spent one year as an Assistant Professor of Religious Studies at Manhattan College in 1969, and served as a visiting professor at the United Theological College, in India, 1972. In 1973 she was appointed as a Lecturer and then Assistant Professor of Theology and Women's Studies at Yale University Divinity School.

While Letty Russell's theological approach and analysis of liberation theology will be the major focus of this chapter, the work of two other theologians, James H. Cone and Gustavo Guiterrez, will be briefly reviewed as representative of two quite different cultural viewpoints out of which liberation theology has arisen. Cone was the first theologian to develop a

systematic black theology based upon the assumption
that Christianity is essentially the liberation of the
oppressed community. Born in 1938 at Fordyce, Arkan-
sas, Cone has rapidly attained a status of theological
prominence through his extensive writings on black
theology. A Professor of Theology at Union Theological Seminary in New York, he has degrees from Phil-
ander Smith College, Garrett Seminary, and Northwestern
University where he took his Ph.D. in 1965. Gutierrez
is professor of theology at the Catholic University in
Peru. A native Peruvian and prominent Catholic Theologian, he serves as advisor to the Latin American
Bishops' Conference and Councilium, and was a resource
expert at the 1968 Medellin Conference. Gutierrez is
most responsible for coining the term "theology of
liberation" and is a mentor of Christian liberation
movements throughout Latin America. The theology of
liberation calls for all Christians to cast their lot
with the oppressed and the poor, and to abolish the
great injustices heaped upon such people by their oppressors, so that they might build a new man and a new
society.

COMMON ELEMENTS

According to Russell feminist theology shares a
number of common elements with Third World theologies
of liberation.[2] However, this is not to say that there
is anything like complete agreement among those people
writing liberation theology.[3] Rather, despite different philosophical and ideological assumptions, the
common experiences of oppression or dehumanization as
a result of sex, race, or class have led these theologians to certain common methodologies. Liberation
theology is above all else a practical theology which
brings together and grows out of action and reflection
(or "praxis"). In this regard its approach is essentially "inductive" rather than deductive. It does not
set out to deduce a system based upon first principles
handed down by Christian tradition, or to create a
great overarching, comprehensive system, but to respond to the life-situations or immediate experiences
of those who have embraced the gospel as "good news."
Liberation theologies recognize that the gospel becomes the good news to the oppressed only when it
speaks concretely to people caught in situations of oppression, whether that be of a racial, sexual, social,
economic, physical or spiritual nature. Therefore, the

inductive method tends to be "experimental" in character — using tentative hypotheses and frequently re-
vising its questions to fit a changing, dynamic environment. In this respect, liberation theology is very dependent upon the support of the community of faith out
of which it develops.[4]

A second commonality, according to Russell, is in
the realm of perspectives. There are at least three
perspectives which liberation theologies hold in common. The first is the conviction that the Biblical
message for this age demands the liberation of all
people. Christians can no longer draw lines of distinction between confessional groups, or Christians
and non-Christians. They must support and join those
who struggle for justice, peace, and freedom wherever
or whoever they may be. The second perspective shared
by liberation theologies is that history takes on meaning as people and the world participate in its processes. In the Bible the world is viewed as moving
through a series of significant events which will ultimately bring about the fulfillment of God's plan for
humankind. The gospel's promise of liberation compels
the Christian to enter into the processes of action and
planning, even into the ideologies that help to change
and shape reality — such as women's liberation, the
black power movement, and Marxism — as means of fur-
thering God's purposes. A third perspective shared by
liberation theologies is that of salvation as total
well-being in community with others. The Old Testament concept of "shalom" (or wholeness) is often used
to emphasize the social character of salvation and
stress is placed upon salvation as a quality of the
here and now. Sin, from this perspective, is interpreted as "oppression," as the opposite of liberation,
as living without wholeness, or community.[5]

Since liberation theologies arise out of the particular situations of oppression in which Christians
find themselves, it is to be expected that numerous
themes would be developed. However, Russell calls
attention to three common themes which tend to unite
the various liberation theologies.[6] The first theme,
which has already been indicated, deals with the central concern of "humanization." What does it mean to
be a human being? What are the key ingredients in the
definition of "human?" Russell insists that the essential factors are the need to be accepted as a sub-

41

ject, not as an object or thing which is always manipulated by others, the need to participate in the shaping and understanding of the world in which the individual finds himself, and the need of a supportive
community. People are known and understood by their
activity in creating their own world and their own
history. The people of the Third World and women
demand the freedom to be known in just this sense.
They refuse to be defined according to the categories
of race, sex, or class. For Christians the sharpest
definition of humanity is to be seen in Christ who
related to people in love regardless of their social
or sexual classification.

A second theme closely allied to the first is the
process of coming to a new consciousness and sense of
responsibility ("conscientization"). According to
Russell, the term conscientization is a term which has
been popularized by the Latin-American theologians to
indicate the continuing process of the importance of becoming aware of the kind of world in which people live
and the constant readiness to take action against all
the oppressive elements of that world. It is a positive program for helping people to develop their own
future.

A third theme which arises out of the search for
liberation and social salvation has to do with "dialogue and community." Dialogue, or mutual trust and
respect, makes possible the development of true community. Liberation theologies do not spend all their
time identifying the oppressed and the oppressors.
Such a procedure would never result in anything better
than reversing the roles of those involved. Liberation
theologies are aware that sin results in barriers of
mistrust between individuals and groups both within
and outside the church. The search for new ways of
dialogue between ministers and laity, whites and
blacks, male and female, rich and poor is taking place
in all liberation theologies. However, dialogue can
take place only within a situation where there is mutual respect and trust. This means that the oppressed groups must first establish a power base, a strong
sense of identity, and the possibility of affective
collective action against the oppressor. At the same
time, it means that the oppressed must develop a positive self-identity, one that is not frustrated by a
sense of inferiority and self-hatred which is simply

the reflection of the existing status quo of the society in which they live. When the oppressed inter-
nalize the subhuman images projected by their society
they only succeed in venting their rage and anger upon
each other. While this often happens, as for instance
when American blacks turned their rage on one another
and burned their own ghetto communities, or when women
become their own worst enemies by becoming radical
supporters of the status quo, it does not further the
cause of dialogue and community. Russell believes
that dialogue becomes possible only when the oppressor and the oppressed begin to envision a shared task
in which they both have some degree of equality in
working with one another. The liberation theologies
are striving to bring about such a transformation of
consciousness, confidence, and leadership among Third
World people and women which will make genuine dialogue possible.

Letty Russell's identification of the common
methods, themes, and perspectives of liberation theologies makes easier the task of seeing the problems
confronting Christians and their societies in the last
quarter of the twentieth century. Simultaneously, it
brings into sharper focus the purpose of those radical
advocates of Black Theology and Feminine Theology by
placing them in a much broader context of concern. At
the same time it raises a warning about the danger of
all theology that tends to become too restrictive in
its concern — who really are "God's elect?"[7] Russell
is completely convinced that liberation theologies are
vital to the life and welfare of the church today. All
the traditional oppressions of people, whether by class,
sex, or race, have been legitimatized and practiced not
only by the hierarchical structures of the church but
by its doctrines and dogmas as well.[8] This despite the
Gospel mandate that Christians must "preach good news
to the poor . . . proclaim release to the captives . . .
set at liberty those who are oppressed." (Luke 4:18)
The liberation theologies are united in their conviction that the church must stop supporting the status
quo and respond to the real heart of the Gospel mandate
for living in a New Age. This thesis is abundantly
articulated by the Latin American theologies of liberation, especially by Gustavo Gutierrez, as well as by
the black theologies, such as that of James Cone.

43

In the opening pages of A Theology of Liberation Gutierrez quotes Edward Schillebeeckx, the well known Belgian born Catholic theologian of the Netherlands, as stating that for centuries the church has concentrated its energies on "formulating truths" while virtually neglecting the task of creating a better world. In other words, the church has been obsessed with its "orthodoxy" but has left "orthopraxis" — the concrete practice of deeds, behavior, and action — in the hands of those outside the Church.[9] For Gutierrez theology is from beginning to end a critical reflection upon the society and the life of the Church, not simply upon its starting points — tradition and revelation. Indeed, reflection on the historical practices ("praxis") — the commitments which Christians, impelled by the Spirit and in fellowship with other people, have undertaken in history — is a liberating theology. Such a theology is not content merely to reflect upon the world, but rather endeavors to become a part of the ongoing process by which the world is changed.[10]

While Gutierrez acknowledges the necessity of the traditional functions of theology — its concern with spiritual growth, and its rational functions of defining truths, examining doctrines, and teaching dogma — he believes that the rediscovery of love as the center of the Christian life has brought about a more Biblical understanding within Catholicism.[11] Faith, when understood as an act of trust, necessitates a total response on the part of man to God — a commitment not just to God, but through love to the neighbor also. The Bible in revealing God to man reveals man's true nature not merely to himself, but to other men as well. The Word of the Bible gathers and is incarnated in the community of the faithful who in turn bestow love in deeds and acts upon others.

Gutierrez believes that the reaffirmation of the Vatican Council II (1962-1965) on the idea of a Church of service rather than power, the philosophy of Maurice Blondel with its stress on the importance of human action, the added influence of Marxist thought with its demand for praxis geared to transform the world, and the rediscovery of the eschatological dimension — the future dimension — in theology have all contributed to a more precise understanding that communion with Christ leads inescapably to a life of concrete commitment of service to others.[12] Indeed, Gutierrez contends that theology must begin with the specific problems and questions raised by the society and the history of a given people. In this way it fulfills a prophetic function by revealing and proclaiming the profound or spiritual significance of these events for its people today. And it also becomes a part of the process which transforms and helps to make history.

A faith which is open to the concrete socio-cultural transformations which are taking place around it cannot remain content with the notion that there are two planes of history or activity — one sacred and the other secular, or one spiritual and the other profane. Rather, man is known historically and concretely as called to meet God, asserts Gutierrez. Salvation cannot be measured in terms of converts to the Church, but only in terms of "qualitative and intensive" fulfillment as a human being.[13] Therefore, liberation theology is committed to the work of transforming this world, this history, since salvation embraces all men and the whole man.

Gutierrez picks up the theme of "liberation" for his theological work because it has come to synthesize the aspirations of the poor and oppressed majorities of Third World countries.[14] However, he points out that the term "liberation" has three levels or dimensions which are reciprocally interpenetrating and which must be dealt with if theology is to avoid the pitfalls of idealism, or spiritualism, and the shallow analyses of that which is merely immediate. At the first level liberation deals with the hopes, needs, and concerns of the oppressed peoples and social classes, whether it be of an economic, political, or social nature. It must deal with those forces which place the oppressed at odds with wealthy nations and other classes. At the second level of liberation a deeper dimension is examined which looks at the way in which man has assumed responsibility for himself throughout his life and across the span of history. The development of true freedom eventually creates a new man and a new society. Finally, on the level of faith, liberation is freedom from sin and communion with God and this provides the basis for true brotherhood.[15]

It is at this third level of the notion of liberation that Gutierrez develops the appropriateness of the term for Christianity and the Church. Liberation opens up a wealth of connections with Biblical sources. In the Bible it is Christ who is presented as the one

who liberates mankind.[16] He liberates man from the ultimate root of all interpersonal disruptions and from
oppression and injustice. He is the one who sets man
free and who enables man to live in communion and harmony with others. St. Paul declared that "for freedom
Christ has set us free" (Gal. 5:1). To the extent that
sin is selfishness, a refusal to love the neighbor, or
Christ himself, it creates the breach of brotherhood.
Such a disruption is the ultimate cause of the injustice, oppression, and poverty in which men live,
according to the Bible.[17]

Having denied the dualistic notion of history (as a
sacred and profane place), Gutierrez insists that the
historical viewpoint concerning the meaning of human
existence rediscovers the Pauline thesis of Christ's
universal lordship.[18] This theme that it is God's will
to bring all men into communion with each other and
with Himself places the emphasis of salvation upon that
which embraces the whole of human reality and leads to
full humanization. "Man," declares Gutierrez, "is des-
tined to total communion with God and to the fullest
brotherhood with all men."[19] Liberation theology,
therefore, does not consider sin as a private, subjective condition of man, but as a social, historical
fact which perpetuates alienation, injustice, oppression, and all the structures of dehumanization. The
basic obstacle to the Kingdom of God is sin. However,
the historical, political liberating events indicate a
growth of the Kingdom, but they are not "all" of salvation or "the" coming of the Kingdom as such. Nevertheless, they are considered as "salvific" events.[20]

For Gutierrez the Church must become a sacrament
of liberation. Its task is to celebrate the salvation
action of God in history and to fulfill the plan of
salvation by making manifest to the world what the
world is to become: a place of true human community
and love. The Church universal plays a unique role in
the process of the humanization of mankind which varies
according to its historical circumstances. However,
Gutierrez believes that the Church itself needs liberation, and he is convinced that if its focus remains
fixed upon the economic and political status quo such
self-liberation will not take place. In Latin America
the renewal of the Church depends upon its solid identification with the exploited, the poor, the marginated
of society. One of its most subtle dangers is that it
will allow itself to become a functional part of the

contemporary system which is trying to suppress some of the most glaring injustices without effecting any radical changes.[21] For Gutierrez, if the theology of liberation does not lead the Church and the Christian community to an active, effective commitment on the part of the exploited and oppressed social classes of Latin America than it will have been of no value.

CONE

James Cone in <u>A Black Theology of Liberation</u> appears to be even more radical than Gutierrez in his insistence upon God's identification with the poor, oppressed, and losers of society. In answer to the question "Why Black Theology?" Cone makes three responses.[22] First of all, he declares that in a polarized society theology can never be neutral. It must be either on the side of the oppressed or on the side of the oppressors, because theology is always identified with a specific community. Secondly, God always takes the side of those who are for goodness and justice. Yahweh takes sides in the Old Testament, and Jesus takes up the cause of the poor and oppressed in the New Testament. This means that God is not color blind in a racist society — which is what exists in America — and is, therefore, on the side of the victims. The victims in America are black people. God who is involved in human history is on the side of black people. Finally, even though, as many liberals will point out, blacks are not the only ones who suffer in this society, the black theologian must take the existential risk of faith and try to discern where God is most active in trying to effect His purpose for the liberation of people from oppression. For the black theologian the most obvious focus and symbol for this liberating activity of God is the black community. "Either God is for black people in their fight for liberation and against the white oppressors, or he is not. He cannot be both for us and for white oppressors at the same time."[23]

Citing Luke 4:18, Cone makes clear from the very beginning of his work that the task of theology is to explicate God's liberating activities on behalf of the oppressed in the world. The meaning of the resurrection-event lies in the fact that God's liberating power is not only for the house of Israel but for all people who are oppressed by principalities and powers. It is a message of hope for the enslaved of mankind

47

which makes them intolerant of present inequities. The task of theology is to proclaim this universal message of hope in God to the particular oppressed community in society in such a way that they will risk all for "earthly freedom."[24] For Cone the universal aspect of the gospel has no meaning unless it can be seen in application to the particular.

Following Paul Tillich's interpretation that the nature of all God-Talk ("theological speech") is symbolic, Cone insists that man must describe God indirectly by symbols that point to the divine or ultimate dimensions of reality. Black Theology keeps symbolic understanding in mind when it speaks, according to Cone. Therefore, "blackness is an ontological symbol" — a symbol of being, of reality — which is not only visible, but which most sharply portrays what oppression, dehumanization, enslavement is all about in America. If the racial minorities of this country wish to destroy the oppressive nature of white society, it can only be done by affirming that identity of being which is anti-white — blackness![25] This "ontological symbol" is the universal aspect of Black Theology which insists that all people were created to be free, and that God is always on the side of the oppressed fighting against the oppressors. Consequently, Cone declares that only that theology which symbolizes God's oppressed people and which speaks for the community of the oppressed, the particular community of Christians who take on this identity, is a "Christian theology." Thus, Christian theology can only mean Black Theology in the black-white struggle.[26]

Cone contends that theology is inseparable from the faith community. Theology presupposes that the reason for the community's being is given at the moment of its birth, and the task which theology has is to make clear to every succeeding generation the relevance of that original truth. For Black Theology this means endeavoring to make clear what knowledge of God means for the blackman in a society which is determined to destroy his very being —both physically, if he asserts his humanity, and symbolically, if he clings to life as simply a nonperson. In such a situation, Cone asserts that "revelation" — God's involvement in history — is the "epistemological justification" of the community's claims for its very survival. As survival theology Black Theology recognizes that by the whiteman's definitions "blackness" is "non-being" — both physically and ontologically. It also recognizes that black survival is dependent upon the blackman's personal identity, as well as his identity with the community which understands, remembers, and interprets its own history. Black Theology seeks to provide the religious dimension of this community's life and history. Black Theology, furthermore, affirms true humanity as blackness in a society in which the oppressor defines the right, the true, the good, and the beautiful in terms of whiteness.[27]

Because Black Theology is survival theology, it is affirmed with passion, with "existential risk." The very meaning and fulfillment of life is at stake. The norm of Black Theology is the identification of God's revelation to the world in the form of an oppressed Jew — Jesus Christ. Christ, as the Oppressed One, becomes the "black Christ." He is the very one, the Oppressed One, whom white society shoots, kills, and bars from humanity. The Black Christ supplies the necessary "soul" for the blackman's humanity or liberation. The Black Christ is the concrete expression of Christ's continued presence today. As biblical tradition makes clear, God's acts in history, His revelation to man, are recognized only by those who have the faith to perceive them. Faith, therefore, is an existential perception of a "situation of oppression" and a commitment to take part in the liberating process revealed by God. It is the community's response to the liberating acts of God.[28] To be free in America is to accept blackness, as the symbol of oppression and the necessity of liberation, and to identify man by the marks of oppression.[29].

What is "sin" for Black Theology? According to Cone it is the separation of man from the source of his identity or being. By rejecting his being man pretends to be what he is not. For the individual man sin, which is a religious concept, is a rejection of the values and goals of the faith community. It is a denial of the community. For the community itself, sin is the recognition that they have lost their very purpose for being. In the case of Israel, it was the forgetting of their covenant with Yahweh which was grounded in the liberating experience of the Exodus — the source of their very being. For Black Theology, sin is the endeavor to "love" or "understand" the whiteman, or enslaver, on his terms. In

49

Black Theology it is only the black perspective, the oppressed perspective, which is qualified to speak about the meaning of sin whether it be for blacks or whites. The only hope for the whiteman to be free, liberated, whole, or saved, is to be created anew in black being. To know God, to know Christ, to be spiritually whole, is to become one with the oppressed.[30] Blackness or salvation is the work or gift of God declares Cone.

RUSSELL

Just as Black Theology and Third World liberation theology have arisen out of the experience of oppression in society so has feminist theology. It is called "feminist theology" because those who do theology in this perspective advocate the equality of the sexes in a society that looks upon women as something a little less than human. Letty Russell calls attention to the fact that the oppression of women by men is the oldest form of human slavery. The subjection of one human being to a permanent status of inferiority on the basis of sex is the most universally practiced form of exploitation and one which has given economic and social support to all other expressions of exploitation both within the church and in the society at large.[31]

The Meaning of Freedom

Russell begins her study of human liberation with an overview of the meaning of "freedom" as a child of God. Her concern is to portray the future possibilities of human development which God holds open for all people. The journey toward freedom is a journey with and for others into God's future. As a universal possibility freedom defies description, definition, or conceptualization. It transcends all definitions or concepts at the moment it is experienced. Consequently, people can only celebrate freedom and perhaps share its new awareness of hope in God's future by some act or word of gratitude. This is why Russell turns to the word "liberation" in her endeavor to describe freedom in the lives of people. She used the concept of liberation not because this word is any more precise than the term "freedom," but because she believes that the term "liberation" brings into sharper focus the ongoing nature of the struggle which people have with

themselves and others as they press for a more open
future for the human race.[32]

Russell confesses that as she seeks to uncover
the possible meanings of freedom it becomes more apparent to her that the search for liberation varies
with each individual and each society. Indeed, like
the promises of God, the promises of human liberation
are never fully known until they are experienced and
even then the immediate experience is transcended by
indications of future possibilities of an even greater
nature. Because of the variable situation of each person who longs to be free from something, or for something, for so many different reasons, Russell believes the only meaningful way to discuss freedom
from a human perspective is in terms of its horizons
as a promise from God.[33]

Taking her cues from the Apostle Paul, especially
his notion of the children of God "groaning" for freedom in the Spirit,[34] Russell contends that Christians
are saved as a part of this "groaning creation" through
"hope." A condition made possible by having already
had a foretaste of the first fruits of the Spirit of
freedom. For those women who have tasted of the frist-
fruits of liberation there is no alternative, but to
demand the total destruction of all dehumanizing social,
political, and economic structures and to become full
participants in the struggles for humanization. For
Christian women, Russell believes that this leads to
a greater responsibility by doing theology. Meeting
together with other women in the function of mutual
consciousness-raising and debate about the problems
is inadequate. Women must search out and clarify the
critical issues and raise the important questions concerning the biblical and ecclesiastical traditions of
the faith. With the gift of the Holy Spirit they must
take prophetic action which will constantly disturb
the status quo attitudes and consciousness of both
church and society.

Citing Jürgen Moltmann's Theology of Hope,
Russell declares that the horizon of Christian freedom
is hope![35] Hope is the expection of those things which
God has given in faith. The freedom and liberation
which the Christ event initiates draws all Christians
into God's action on behalf of human liberation. It
draws people into the "horizon" of God's hope for
humankind. And this horizon, in keeping with the

nature of a horizon, is constantly changing as it is approached, as Christians journey together toward God's future. The question of the Christian, says Russell, is not "When will justice, peace, freedom and human dignity be attained?" but "How can Christians live now as though it had been attained?"[36] This means that the idea of liberation is not just some passing fancy for Christians. Rather, it is the recognition that God's future, the horizon of freedom, will be an imperative upon Christians long after liberation theologies or liberation movements have faded away. Christians living in the horizon of freedom are hoping against hope in God's future; they are anticipating that future in the present in some small measure.[37]

By living in anticipation of God's future (Paul's "proleptic" emphasis), Russell insists that Christians can become "signs" which contradict all patterns of dehumanization, oppression, injustice, and human conflict. By living the life-style of co-humanity now in home, church, and society men and women become a prolepsis (an "anticipation") of the way of life in God's future. For Russell the Christian mandate is to live out the way of freedom now!

Finding a Meaningful Past

As indicated earlier, Russell defines the process of coming to true humanity as having three important ingredients. First, a person must, to some extent, participate in the understanding and shaping of his or her world and its future. Second, every person needs a supportive community in which to discover himself or herself. Third, every person needs to be accepted by other persons and themselves as subjects not objects.[38] Russell believes that the praxis of liberation theology — which seeks to reflect upon the love of God, as seen in Christ, as the basis of the future — can help immensely in working out the social and biblical patterns that endeavor to overcome human oppression and dislocation. Before an oppressed people can enter into a shaping of their own future, they must discover some understanding of history on which to structure their future — what Russell calls a "usable past."[39] Recent discussions in the ecumenical efforts of Roman Catholics and Protestants have led them to discover some common understandings about the nature of written and unwritten tradition. Schol-

52

ars of both groups have now begun to make distinctions within the meaning of the word "tradition." According to Russell, distinctions are now being made by many theologians between "traditions" of a given confessional group and "Tradition" as God's deliverance of Jesus as the Christ.[40] However, Russell follows a three fold distinction of tradition set forth by the Faith and Order Commission of the World Council of Churches study which, completed in 1963, deals with "tradition, traditions, and the Tradition."[41]

She notes that "tradition" is a basic human category which focuses upon change as the instrument of human life. This understanding of tradition is very important for oppressed peoples because it turns away from the attitude of former generations who thought of tradition as a repository of the past and focuses upon the shaping of events which are meaningful for the present and the future. The view of history which understands tradition as a tool by which people may sift out those myths and interpretations which have perpetuated the status quo is of great value to liberation theology. When tradition can be understood as a process by which people come to an awareness of themselves and the world in order to shape their present and the future, a more humane and usable future is open to all.[42]

When a new look is taken at "the Tradition" and "traditions" in the light of the new understanding of "tradition," as discussed above, Russell believes that it can be seen that all belong to the same theological spectrum. The handing over of Jesus, as the Christ ("the Tradition"), is a part of God's plan to redeem humanity; the participation of the church in its various confessional forms ("traditions") by its sending or missionary activity through a shaping of the present and the future becomes a part of the sending activity of God; men and women aware of the meaningful mission of God to lead all people to the truth commit themselves to molding the present and the future ("tradition").[43] Consequently, for Russell it is possible to say that "Tradition is Mission." God's mission in the handing over of Christ into the hands of humankind in order that all people may know the truth throughout history becomes the means by which men and women in every generation and nation participate in God's mission and the Tradition. By participating in the receiving and passing on of this tradition people participate in God's purpose to bring about a "new creation" in which Christ will bring all things, including himself, back to God.[44]

This understanding of Tradition as Mission is, according to Russell, a key concept in liberation theologies. Just as in the past God has broken into history to liberate people from oppressive human conditions, so in this Tradition as Mission the theme of a usable past which points towards a hope in God's future opens up the possibility of joining God's traditioning process. Such a possibility means, for liberation theologies, finding a usable language and useful actions which will allow the gospel to be heard and seen as good news in every generation and for all people.

Russell notes that various expressions of liberation theology are seen as a threat by those "confessional traditions" which do not wish to see their tradition challenged by new ways. This, for instance, is true of those traditions which have perpetuated an unusable past for a particular group within Christendom — whether it be the right of women to function as priests, or the refusal to admit certain ethnics into full fellowship. It is, also, true of those traditions which regard their past as a "deposit of faith," as a body of content which must be protected by some authorized hierarchy.[45] Liberation theologies insist that God's mission throughout tradition is to make Christ's love applicable in the lives of all people and to bring about freedom, justice, peace, equality, and reconcilation for all. Russell declares that liberation theology stands as a reminder of the fact that God's Tradition stands in judgment over all human endeavors.

Since tradition and traditions have been misused as a way of legitimatizing the power base of the Western, white, male majority, liberation theologies are compelled to recover the true Biblical meaning of God's Tradition and the traditions. However, finding a usable past may prove to be very difficult for some people within a culture, not simply because of the lack of identity as a group and the ego strength to face the pressures of life, but because that past has systematically been distorted by the dominant oppressor

54

who has written and recorded that past. Russell notes
that this is a special problem for women and Third
World people. Women particularly often have no awareness of their own past as a group because their roles
and functions in history have been interpreted, for the
most part, by men, and because they have no cultural
tradition of their own. This means that women in history are frequently invisible.[46]

Following Gerhard Ebeling's interpretation of
"history" — as a self-definition and description of
reality — Russell notes that it includes much more
than a mere critical research into the record of the
past.[47] History also includes a narrative of events
which continue to have meaning for those involved in
the original events — such as "Tradition" — as well
as for those who are existentially creating their own
tradition today. Even though church history and
traditions, having been recorded and interpreted by
the dominate male victors of the past, have systematically excluded the views of the schismatics and the oppressed, Russell contends that the contributions of
minorities are not entirely obscured. Indeed, biblical records include an abundance of material pertaining to the long and complex history of people's reaction to the liberating acts of God.[48] In the Old Testament, for instance, one of the causes for the strong
patriarchal tradition with its emphasis upon male images of Yahweh is due to the intense conflict with the
Canaanite fertility gods. In New Testament writings,
especially in the works of Paul and the Gospels, despite the restricted role and status of women in the
Jewish culture at that time the full human status of
women is attested to by both Paul and Jesus.

Of the numerous examples cited by Russell concerning the attitude of Jesus toward women, the story
of the Samaritan woman is very instructive. Jewish
men were forbidden to speak to women in public at that
time, and associating with Samaritans who were their
bitter religious enemies was unthinkable, yet Jesus
treated the woman with love and concern as he would
any other person. Women were counted among his followers (Luke 8:1-3) and were the first to proclaim his
resurrection which was handed on as "the Tradition"
to the disciples and others (Luke 24:1-11). Russell
notes that Paul recognized that "the Tradition" was
handed over to both men and women (I Cor. 11:2-16),
as were the gifts of the Holy Spirit (I Cor. 12;6;

14:26-36), and that Paul recognized that Christ had
ushered in a New Age which would make no distinction
between slave and free, Greek and Jew, male and female
(Gal. 3:28).

Russell believes that myths, also, must be ex-
plored by liberation theologies in the search for a
usable history. Even though myths may contain many useless elements for those oppressed peoples seeking to
find a usable past, unexamined myths, especially the
common social myth, may actually perpetuate the dehumanizing prejudices of the status quo. False social
myths, such as "Negroes have small brains," "The poor
are lazy," and "Women are bad professional risks,"
need to be destroyed by the real facts of life. Nevertheless, myths have and continue to have an important
place in shaping the human condition. As Biblical theologians, such as Bultmann, have pointed out the Judaeo-
Christian faith was formed in a mythical world tradition
and can only be understood in the light of this world-
view. The etiological myths of Genesis, chapters 1 to
11, for example, continue to have theological truths
which have significance for those who affirm the Tradition of God.[49]

An important aspect of the search for a usable
history on the part of oppressed peoples, whether they
be blacks, women, or the poor, is a critical examination of language. Language reflects the conscious and
unconscious values and social patterns of a people and
their culture, and, therefore, is an important tool not
only in maintaining the status quo but in molding and
shaping the future of a people. For those whose lives
have been dehumanized because of biological or racial
origin, language is just one more instrument that has
been used to exclude them from history and myth and a
meaningful future. Russell notes that to counteract
this fact of life, many Third World peoples have returned to the dialects, traditions, and expressions of
their own culture as a medium for affirming their human
uniqueness. Within women's liberation movements the
task of "desexing language" has become a major concern.
Finding human pronouns to replace the so called "gen-
eric" pronouns of man, men, his, brotherhood, etc.,
has become increasingly important as a way of counter-
ing the male-dominated society.

The problem of a male-dominated language is no-
where more pervasive than in the Judaeo-Christian re-

ligious life. Finding a usable language for the educa-
tional and worship experiences of the church is one of
the real challenges confronting feminist theology. Not
only are women excluded from many of the roles in the
hierarchy of the church, their very existence is denied
by most of the references used in liturgies, hymns,
traditions, and Biblical and theological language about
God and humankind. The search for new forms of expression of God, and the people of God, must begin with the
interpretation of the Tradition as found in the Biblical record. Russell believes that Biblical tradition
makes it very clear that God's reality is a mystery
which cannot be described by metaphor or image except
as that mystery is revealed by its saving activity in
history. Therefore, "God language should not be confused with the reality of God, . . ."[50] The first
order of business for feminist theology is to uncover
God's reality through careful study and interpretation.
Some of this reality can be seen in God's "forgotten
names."[51]

Despite the fact that many of the characteristics
ascribed to God in earliest traditions included both
male and female features, Russell points out that these
characteristics were increasingly replaced by male
features. This process was probably accelerated, she
notes, after the Babylonian exile when women came to be
considered as "ritually unclean." In spite of this
antifeminine bias the present Biblical form and ecclesial traditions reveal some images of God which were
and still are accepted as feminine in character. The
image of God as servant or helper ('ezer) found in
Exodus, chapter 3, is very important as it is seen in
relationship to God's characteristic as servant found
in Genesis, chapter 2, in which the creation story of
Eve appears as the helper ('ezer) of Adam.[52] The fact
that this image of servant is taken up by Jesus in the
New Testament (Mark 10:45) and becomes a distinctive
mark of his identification by Paul and the Gospel writers, adds weight to its theological importance.[53] The
Genesis 1:26 account, which speaks of the creation of
humankind as "male and female" in the "image" of God,
Russell believes is important along with the plural
word used for God in that context (Elohim) which reflects the idea that God (Yahweh) combines both the
male and female characteristics of the Canaanite pan-
theon.[54] Other examples cited by Russell are the
images of God as acting like the mother bird protecting

her young, comparing God's love to a mother's love for her child, or a wife's love for her husband.

Finally, Russell calls attention to those Biblical passages, and a few orthodox theological traditions, which speak of the functions of the Spirit of God (the use of the feminine gender, ruach, in the Hebrew) as feminine, and the interrelationship of the Trinity as having both male and female characteristics. Russell insists that at this time in history it would be wise for the church and its theologians to make use of those images and metaphors of God, and the Godhead, which portray both male and female as a way of making clear that the Tradition is for all people — not just the male half. She also believes it would be wise at this moment in time to speak of the Holy Spirit strictly in female terms. Liberation theologies must continue to search God's Tradition for its usable future, history, and language in order that this Tradition will speak meaningfully to all people.

Finding Support in Community

However, in addition to understanding and shaping their own worlds, people need supportive communities in which to discover themselves if they are to attain full humanity. Because of their commitment to the praxis methodology, liberation theologies are led to doing and telling liberation. They seek to tell the good news of God's gift of salvation and freedom in such a way that the oppressed will actually experience it in their everyday lives. This has led to a reflection upon the meaning of God's liberation and freedom in particular situations of oppression, and to a focus upon the Biblical message of salvation for humankind.

Russell stressed the fact that liberation theologies have returned to the themes of liberation and blessing as the key concepts of Biblical salvation. The goal of salvation for the Hebrew people was "shalom," a word which embraced a wide variety of meanings including peace, wholeness, prosperity, social, family, and personal well-being.[55] The Old Testament motif of "liberation" focuses upon deliverance from sin, death, suffering, imprisonment, and distress while the motif of "blessing" calls attention to the positive powers of life given by God for wholeness and goodness in creation and creature. Russell points out that the liberating act of God, as a past event and as a prom-

58

ised hope, is all included in the concept of <u>shalom</u> and that the overlapping themes of deliverance and blessing are seen in the New Testament in Jesus who came as the "Prince of Shalom."[56] Through his healings (blessing) and by his crucifixion and resurrection (liberation) Jesus fulfills God's promise of salvation for humankind.

However, in the writings of Paul and in the later epistles of the New Testament the word most frequently used for salvation, <u>soteria</u>, reduces its import for the broader social relations and deals primarily with the individual divine-human encounter. According to Russell, this tendency toward restricting the meaning of salvation even farther continues in the early period of church history, primarily as a result of the Hellenistic notion of the separation of body and soul.[57] An identical restriction on the connotation of "sin" can be traced throughout the Biblical account and the later church traditions.[58]

Liberation theologies having returned to the broader concept of salvation — as embracing both motifs of liberation and blessing — see liberation not just as God's gift in the Tradition, but as the major agenda of all the oppressed who join together in community to transform society. They see liberation as the goal of complete social and physical wholeness in which freedom is really possible. They see blessing as "humanization" in which full personhood can be realized in community with others. And "sin," while not denying individual accountability, is understood most forcefully as a refusal to give Third World people and women room to breathe, to hope for a greater future, and to live as human beings in society.[59]

Letty Russell believes that women are very much interested in the reinterpretation of sin as understood by liberation theologies. No only has sin been given the extremely one-sided individualistic interpretation in church tradition, beginning with the Adam and Eve story sin has been associated with women and sex. Sin has stressed, also, a predominantly male perspective by its emphasis upon a "will-to-power," <u>hubris</u> (pride), lust, and aggression. Whereas, the greater temptations and sin of women may lie more in the realms of "dependence on others," "underdevelopment or negation" of the self, and "triviality."[60]

Despite the oppressive nature of the hierarchical structures of the church and, especially, its white, male, Western imperialism, Russell is convinced that liberation theologies cannot forsake the church because it is the very womb or matrix out of which praxis theology is nurtured. As people seek to reflect on the world in the light of God's Tradition, God's action in the world, they must relate to the witnessing community of faith. Liberation theologians must always strive to make the church be the church.[61] The search for liberation and blessing which moves toward the goal of complete personhood in community with others (shalom) cannot ignore human tradition or God's Tradition. In both instances people may discover signs of wholeness which will make possible the act of opening themselves up to a new reality.

Russell cites as examples, of the way in which God's Mission through Christ is handed over to the actions of men and women of all generations and nations, the similarities between "conscientization" and "conversion" and "praxis" and "evangelism."[62] The Biblical and ecclesial tradition have many stories about the dramatic conversions of people which lead them to adopt new names and new lifestyles. Liberation theologians point out that the same kind of process happens among oppressed peoples as a result of consciousness-raising (conscientization).[63] A whole new understanding of the meaning of life, a radical reorientation or transformation, often takes place in the lives of women or Third World people as a result of conscientization. Just as the experience of conscientization leads people to a greater sense of wholeness and grace, so does the continuing effort of participating in God's Mission by the church lead to new levels of action and reflection. The task of evangelism is that of doing and telling. It is not a program that is to be accomplished but goes on continually. It grows out of participation in God's love for humankind and has the goal of shalom for all humanity. The task of the church is "to point to Christ in the world and not to itself."[64]

Russell believes that liberation theologians need to work together with others to make the church free for its "true" purpose of carrying forth God's work in the world. Before the church can become a truly supportive community for all those Third and Fourth World peoples seeking full humanity, it must participate in dialogue with them by action and reflection. There can

be little openness for the world on the part of the
church until it experiences solidarity with the alienated and suffering marginal peoples. However, such
participation and community is always possible, declares Russell, because Christ's presence with his people creates koinonia (fellowship, communion, sharing).[65]
For Russell the most likely approach to real "dialogue"
— the consequence of true communion and participation
of people with God through Christ and the Holy Spirit —
is through "open ecclesiology." By open ecclesiology
she means that the church ceases to focus directly upon
itself and focuses, instead, upon God and his creatures
by opening itself up to "the world, to others, and to
the future."[66] She is convinced that only when Christians understand salvation as a social and as an individual event, and begin to deal with the social issues
that are obstacles to communication will the church
really become the church.

As for the traditional concept of the ministry in
the church, Russell points out that it is already symbolic of the most oppressive structures of church life
("vertical violence"), and is undergoing a real identity crises as a result of both male and female concern
over its meaning and purpose in a world calling for
greater participation and liberation for all people.
Most of the proposed new "models" for ministry appear
to be no more satisfying than those of the past.[67] Her
own proposal taken from the model of Christ, as the
Suffering Servant (diakonia), poses problems for women
as well as others.

Finding the Person

The third important aspect for coming to true
humanity recognized by Russell is to be accepted by
others, as well as yourself, as a subject and not as an
object. Genuine community exists, and genuine dialogue
emerges where people share life and all are viewed as
persons. While the search for a full humanity takes
place in discovering a usable past, and a meaningful
present, its basic thrust is towards the future. Russell insists that "the truly human is also the newly
human; the vision of new righteousness, peace, and justice in community."[68] Even though this search begins
in the Old Testament, with its vision of a restored
people living in shalom, it continues most forcefully
for liberation theology in the New Testament understanding of Jesus Christ as the New Humanity.

The testimony given by the authors of the New Testament is that God entered into and changed humanity decisively in the person of Jesus Christ. Jesus Christ now becomes the representative of God's intention for all people who can come to know the truth about themselves and their future under God through Christ. Russell believes that if women take their stand with Christ, as God's "Representative," it must be made clear that his work was, first of all, that of being human and not male.[69] She insists that Christian women see Jesus as one who helped both men and women to understand that real personhood displays acceptance, love, compassion, and caring by both sexes. His life demonstrated that he was a whole person whose primary concern was to affirm others as persons, as subjects, and to hold open to others the same possibilities for personhood. Therefore, feminist theology cannot think of Christ first of all in terms of his male sex or his racial origin (the "scandal" of his Jewish particularity) for to do so would be to affirm those very characteristics about people which Jesus saw as secondary. The most important affirmation about Jesus as the Christ is his pro-humanity.[70]

As the representative of the New Humanity, those who participate with Christ through faith take on the responsibility of helping to bring liberation and blessing into the lives of all people. Russell maintains that the Biblical model for the achievement of this goal is that of the Suffering Servant (the ebed Yahweh hymns of the Old Testament, Isaiah 42:1; 53:12, and the diakonia of the New Testament, Matthew 12:15-21; 17:9-13).[71] The servant role is one of honor and responsibility designated for all men and women who accept God's challenge to take part in his work and service in the world. The role is clearly identified with Jesus in the Gospels and in the Pauline writings of the New Testament the word "apostle" carries the same implication. Representatives of the New Humanity, the true humanity, are to follow the example of Jesus by living a life of love and service to God and others.

However, the role of a servant presents real problems to women and other oppressed groups whose primary experiences of dehumanization are the results of being forced into servant roles. The humanizing experiences for these people, declares Letty Russell, is not performing services for others, but experiencing self-affirmation and hope in genuinely supportive communities. For women this is experienced in the process of "sisterhood." In a male dominated culture and church where the idea of "servant" is associated with power-lessness and subordination, the real "scandal" of the role of the servant, which is the only consistent form of power in the church, is that of "suffering." The dehumanized peoples of the world and the church are already suffering and have suffered enough! Women's liberation, and liberation theology, seeks to destroy the power structures of both church and society which suppress the development of genuine sisterhood and com-munity. Until women have learned to accept their own identities as women, and have learned to work out their own life styles in church and society with other women, they will not be free to be God's servants with or for others.[72]

While the Christian community is called to be a visible symbol of the New Humanity under God, where new life-styles, partnerships, and community may emerge and exist, where true servanthood prevails, such will not be the case until Christians and the sisterhood of women reflect upon and act against all the dehumanizing structures of society. So long as the domination-sub-jugation, authority-submission social patterns prevail in society, and especially between men and women, women cannot be fully human. So long as sex is thought to be the exclusive self-definition of women, so long as women cannot enter fully into the economic, political, and social shaping of the world with men they will not gain full human identity. The feminist theologian is de-termined to gain full human dignity, and she sees the praxis of liberation theology as a method which can as-sist her in her fight against human dislocation and op-pression.[73]

In contrast to cultural or story theology, lib-eration theology focuses sharply upon the Biblical and ecclesiastical heritage of the Christian faith. Its sources for doing theology are very traditional, but its interpretation of those sources in view of the con-temporary issues confronting Christians supplies its radical character. Liberation theology would appear to be addressing a much larger perspective of concern than cultural theology does even though its focus is at times upon minority groups within Western culture. While it makes almost exclusive claims for its inter-pretation of Christ, the question it raises as to what is the "good news" of the Gospel for the oppressed,

suffering, and downtrodden peoples of the earth cannot
be avoided by the serious Christian. While liberation
theology may at times express too much optimism about
human possibilities, and place too much emphasis upon
communal salvation, it is a needed corrective perhaps
for the white, male dominated traditional theology of
radical sinfullness and individuality. Even though
the liberation theologian may be accused of uniting the
good news of God's liberation too closely with the
classless socialistic society, of a Marxian type of
socialism, the concern to live the full life here and
now without fear of punishment or hopes for rewards
in the next life inserts a healthy realism into Christianity.

[1](The Westminster Press, 1974). This author is greatly indebted to the analysis and insights of Ms. Russell for his own current understanding of the topic of liberation theology.

[2]The term "Third World" is used to refer to those people who live outside the United States and Western Europe (people of the "First World") and those who live outside of the Communist bloc countries, or Eastern Europe (people of the "Second World"). It also includes the descendents of the "Third World" who live in racial oppression regardless of country. In North America it refers also to those "nonwhites" who constitute about two-thirds of the world's people but who are socially, economically, and politically oppressed. Women are sometimes referred to as the "Fourth World" when thought of as an oppressed people despite the fact that they make up the sexual majority in the world's population. See Russell, Human Liberation in a Feminist Perspective -- A Theology (The Westminster Press, 1974), pp. 20-21. Hereafter cited as Human Liberation.

[3]Indeed, Francis P. Fiorenza takes exception to Russell's classification of Jürgen Moltmann, Johannes Metz and Dorothee Sölle and argues for a distinction between "political" and "liberation" theologies. See Fiorenza, "Political Theology and Liberation Theology: an inquiry into their fundamental meaning," pp. 3-29, and Russell, "Liberation Theology in a Feminist Perspective," pp. 88-107, especially, p. 90, in Liberation, Revolution, and Freedom: Theological Perspectives, ed. Thomas McFadden (Seabury Press, 1975).

[4]Cf. Russell, Human Liberation, pp. 50-56; also "Liberation Theology in a Feminist Perspective," loc. cit., pp. 91-92.

[5]Cf. Russell, Human Liberation, pp. 56-62; also "Liberation Theology in a Feminist Perspective," pp. 92-95.

[6]Cf. Human Liberation, pp. 63-71.

[7]Russell notes that liberation theology tends to become what Martin Marty has called "genetive theologies: theologies of women, of blacks, of Latin Americans, etc." See ibid, pp. 52-53.

[8]See ibid., pp. 70-71.

[9]Cf. A Theology of Liberation, tr. and ed. by Caridad Inda and John Eagleson (Orbis Books, 1973), p. 10.

[10]See ibid., p. 15.
[11]See ibid., pp. 6-7.
[12]See ibid., pp. 8-11.
[13]See ibid., chs. Four, Five, Nine, especially,
pp. 56-58; 71-72; 150-152.
[14]Cf. ibid., ch. Two, especially, pp. 22-27, 32.
[15]See ibid., pp. 25-37; 176-178; cf., also, pp.
232-239.
[16]See ibid., chs. Nine and Ten.
[17]See ibid., pp. 35, 152, 175, 295.
[18]See ibid., pp. 71, 150.
[19]Ibid., p. 198.
[20]See ibid., pp. 176-177.
[21]Cf. ibid., chs. Seven, Twelve, and Thirteen,
especially, pp. 265-279; 300-302.
[22]Cf. A Black Theology of Liberation (J. B. Lippincott Company, 1970), pp. 25-27.
[23]Ibid., p. 27. Cone maintains the same radical
position in his most recent book, God of the Oppressed
(The Seabury Press, 1975).
[24]See ibid., pp. 20-22.
[25]See ibid., pp. 27-29. Note especially Cone's
footnote on pp. 28-29.
[26]See ibid., pp. 32-33. Cf., also, his discussions
on man in ch. V, especially, pp. 155-159, 168-172, 182-
184, 186-190, 192-194; and his discussions about the
Christ in ch. VI, especially, pp. 202-203, 205, 208-
209, 212-216, 218-219; and the church, ch. VII, especially, pp. 230-234, 237, 243.
[27]See ibid., pp. 30-31, 34-44, 83-85, 90-92, 95,
98-100, 104.
[28]See ibid., pp. 45-49, 74-81, 92-95, 155-159, et.
passim.
[29]See ibid., p. 183. See also the excellent
article by Cone, "Freedom, History, and Hope," in
Liberation, Revolution, and Freedom: Theological
Perspectives, pp. 59-74.
[30]See ibid., pp. 98-100, 120-125, 186-196.
[31]See Russell, Human Liberation, p. 29, and
especially notes 9, 10, and 11.
[32]See ibid., pp. 25-27.
[33]See ibid., pp. 25, 33-38, 41-48.
[34]See Romans 8:14-27; II Cor. 3:17; 1:22; Gal.
3:23-29.
[35]See Human Liberation, p. 41, notes 30, 32.
[36]Cf. ibid., p. 42. This becomes the major subject
of her chapters 4 and 5.

[37]See _ibid._, pp. 41-47.
[38]See _ibid._, p. 132.
[39]See _ibid._, ch. 3.
[40]See _ibid._, pp. 74-78.
[41]See _ibid._, p. 75 and notes 3 and 4. See, also, Russell's discussion of some of this same material in her article "Liberation Theology in a Feminist Perspective," _loc. cit._, pp. 98-104.
[42]See _ibid._, pp. 75-76.
[43]Cf. _ibid._, pp. 76-78, and "Liberation Theology in a Feminist Perspective," _loc. cit._, pp. 100-102.
[44]Russell cites Matt. 24:14 and I Cor. 15:24-28, as support for this interpretation.
[45]Cf. _Human Liberation_, pp. 78-80, also, "Liberation Theology in Feminist Perspective," _loc. cit._, pp. 102-104.
[46]See _Human Liberation_, pp. 80-85.
[47]See _ibid._, pp. 15, 82-84. Russell follows the distinctions made by Ebeling of history as "Historie" — a chronicle of the facts, "Geschichte" — events which continue to have relevance for those involved in the events, and "Geschichtlichkeit" — events which have meaning for people _now_. Russell notes that these same categories of history can be used in reference to tradition. "Historie," as a story of the facts, is reflected in the "traditions" of the church. "Geschichte," as a reference to the meaning of the original events and their interpretation by the faith community, is reflected in "Tradition." And "Geschichtlichkeit," as a reference to all that material of tradition which has existential or vital meaning for Christians today as that which shapes their present and future, is reflected in "tradition."
[48]See _ibid._, pp. 85-89.
[49]See _ibid._, pp. 89-93.
[50]_Ibid._, p. 98.
[51]See _ibid._, pp. 97-103.
[52]Cf. _ibid._, pp. 98-99.
[53]See Russell's discussion of "_Diakonia_" (servant) _ibid._, pp. 30-33; 140-145.
[54]See _ibid._, p. 99.
[55]See _ibid._, pp. 106-107.
[56]See _ibid._, pp. 107-108.
[57]See _ibid._, p. 108.
[58]See _ibid._, p. 109.
[59]See _ibid._, pp. 110-113.
[60]See _ibid._, pp. 112-113.

[61]See _ibid._, ch. 6.

[62]See _ibid._, pp. 121-130.

[63]The term "Conscientization" is a term popularized by a Third World educator, Paulo Freire, and is
used extensively by Gutierrez and other liberation
theologians. Besides emphasizing the whole process
of "consciousness-raising," it implies cultural action and the process of action-reflexion (_praxis_)
See Russell, _ibid._, pp. 114-117, especially, notes
33, 34.

[64]Ibid., p. 127.

[65]See _ibid._, pp. 156-157.

[66]See _ibid._, pp. 157-172.

[67]See _ibid._, pp. 172-182. She does suggest that
there are three models of ministry that might be ex-
plored with profit in the concepts of "advocates,"
"mother, or nurturer," and "lay-person" in the sense
of its variety of roles. (See pp. 180-181).

[68]Ibid., p. 133.

[69]See _ibid._, p. 138.

[70]Cf. _ibid._, pp. 139, 144, 153.

[71]See _ibid._, pp. 140-142; 30-33, for additional
references.

[72]Cf. _ibid._, pp. 142-145.

[73]See _ibid._, pp. 145-154.

CHAPTER THREE

PROCESS THEOLOGY

For the past three decades there have been a group
of theologians in this country engaged in the task of
interpreting Christian doctrines by the use of such concepts as "becoming," "process," "change," "participation," "organic," "emergence," and "dynamic." These
and many other terms of an even more technical nature
have been used in an attempt to appropriate the Process
Philosophy of Alfred North Whitehead for the Christian
community.

WHITEHEAD

Whitehead who was born in Ramsgate, England, in
1861, was the son of a clergyman in the Church of
England and the brother of a well known bishop in
India. As a boy he was greatly influenced by his
father's preaching and teaching. He remained at Ramsgate until he was fourteen being taught both Latin and
Greek by his father. He continued his study in these
subjects and added history, particularly Roman and
Greek history, and especially mathematics at Sherborne.
In 1880 he entered Trinity College, Cambridge, England,
where he concentrated in mathematics. However, due to
influence of friends and family background he, also,
developed a keen interest in philosophy, religion,
politics and especially literature. In 1910 he resigned his position as Senior Lecturer in Mathematics at
the University of Cambridge and moved to London, where
he became engaged in writing, teaching, and adminis-
trative work at the University of London.

Whitehead was preparing for retirement from teaching when he received an invitation from Harvard University, in Cambridge, Massachusetts, to teach philosophy.
This invitation to teach general philosophy apparently
came as a surprise to Whitehead since he had spent his
life working primarily in the area of philosophy of
science. However, this move to Harvard in 1924 gave
him the opportunity to develop his most creative and
systematic thought which he gave expression to in such
works as Process and Reality (1929), The Function of
Reason (1929), Science and the Modern World (1926),
Adventures of Ideas (1933), Modes of Thought (1938),

and Religion in the Making (1929).[1] Even more important it was in this country that Whitehead gained the scholarly recognition which led to a critical examination of his thought and its further development and presentation by disciples. Professor Charles Hartshorne, who taught philosophy at the University of Chicago for more than a quarter of a century, has argued most vigoriously and eloquently for "process-thought."[2] It was his influence which attracted many of the first generation of theologians to process-thought, such men as Professors Daniel Day Williams, Bernard M. Loomer, W. Norman Pittenger, and Bernard Meland, as well as second generation theologians such as Professors Schubert Ogden and John B. Cobb.

What is Process Philosophy all about? Why is it that some theologians find it so attractive as a philosophical basis for Christian apologetics? The first of these two questions can be answered only in a very sketchy manner. It is hoped that the answers given in response to the second question, and particularly the presentation of the main ideas of John B. Cobb, Jr., will make clearer the nature of process-thought.

Perhaps the simplest and most readable of Whitehead's books is Modes of Thought. For anyone who desires to get into a good introduction of Whitehead's developed philosophy this work is the place to start. However, Whitehead felt obliged to develop a very technical language in order to express his sense of the processive, organic nature of reality. As a philosopher he was greatly concerned that his ideas be presented consistently, coherently, and above all logically and rationally. His system of ideas is presented most tightly in Process and Reality where, by his consistent examination of experience as a whole, he presents "realities" not directly experienced but affirmed by a sense of orderliness and coherence. Every generalization must be constantly tested, according to Whitehead, by reference back to the specific given evidence which has been studied, observed, or experienced in the various fields of interest.[3] Briefly, what are the basic notions pertaining to the nature of reality (or what philosophers would call the metaphysical scheme) as understood by process philosophy?

Basic Notions of Process

First, nothing exists in total isolation.[4] Everything is related to some degree, directly or indirectly, to every other thing or entity. Nothing exists except by participation. The universe, the cosmos, is one gigantic network of interconnected events and mutual influences. Man is no exception biologically, mentally, or socially. The hydrogen, oxygen, nitrogen, carbon, and minute traces of other elements which go into the makeup of the human body are the stuff of the stars. There is no dualism of body and mind as Descarte believed. The body is affected by the mind and the mind is affected by the body. The person is precisely the product of his interaction with other persons in society. There is a continuity to the whole of creation from the most abstract sub-atomic particle to the molecule, the cell, the organ, the organism, and society. There is a continuity of interconnected events and mutual influences that characterize every entity from the inorganic to the organic to the psychic. The world is seen holistically as a unity despite its many parts.

Secondly, nothing is static in the universe either at the inorganic or the organic level.[5] The basic analogy for understanding is not the machine but the organism.[6] What the macrocosm and the microcosm of our environment present to us is a highly integrated and interrelated dynamic process. Everything is evolving, changing, emerging, developing or disintegrating. Man is not confronted by unchanging substances with mere changing attributes, as Aristotle perceived the world. Rather, all is change! If man could focus a motion picture camera upon the landscape for a million years and then play it back in five minutes time, he would see mountains rise, fall, and erode like drifting sand and trees sprout, grow, and die in a fraction of a second. Time is a primary factor in the way man understands his universe which is in the process of evolving, flux, and becoming. What the scientist observes and attempts to describe are the continual changes of matter whether in the explosions of the supernovas in distant galaxies or the constant renewal and death of living cells in the human body. Reality is in process.

Thirdly, reality exhibits novelty, spontaniety, and self-creation.[7] Out of the emerging events of the universe, out of its great plurality and variety, its many parts and forms, new creations, unpredictable occurrences, spontaneous developments take place. What under an older philosophy would have been called a chain of cause and effect is seen here as being much more complicated and involved. Reality as an interwoven network of dynamic complex events is constantly giving birth to new syntheses of events. Process philosophy assigns a prominent role to the aims, the goals, the purposes, the ends (the teleology) of events. God himself is possessed of such aims for His creation. The interpenetrating sequence of events in nature which, for example, give rise to new levels of adaptation by an organism, contributes something distinctively different to the life processes. The same kinds of novelty take place at every level of reality. This means that there is a kind of real openness for the future. Man, especially, is able to contribute or add something to creation as it continues.

Its Appeal For Theologians

Why do some theologians find process philosophy so attractive as a basis for Christian apologetics? Perhaps the greatest appeal of Whitehead's philosophy for the theologian is that it presents a metaphysical picture of the universe which appears highly compatible with contemporary scientific knowledge but one which, at the same time, presupposes and incorporates the idea of God. Divine power is stressed but is qualified by immanence within the processes of reality. God, for Whitehead, is the "primordial" example of all reality principles;[8] he embodies the potential forms of orderly relationship even before they are brought into actuality. But, God, also, has a "consequent nature" which means that He is influenced by events in the world.[9] (Both of these concepts will be looked at later in this chapter.)

Another attractive feature of process philosophy is that it pictures God as the source of novelty and creativity in our world.[10] This seems to allow greater possibilities for nature, as well as for man to work out higher ideals and values within life. Some process theologians would contend that this view is much more in keeping with the Biblical view of God and is, therefore, to be preferred.[11] It means that the whole of creation is open at every point to the action of God--that creation continues. It means that God-- as the Supremely Related One--is Love; that this Love pulls man toward communion, not only with God, but community with his fellowmen. It means that man has greater freedom to work out God's purpose with Him in temporality.[12]

Process thought has gained tremendous support in recent years among those theologians endeavoring to work out a stronger theological relationship between man and nature. Man's growing concern about his natural environment--the ecological concern--has made necessary a reexamination by Christians of their attitudes about stewardship of nature. The traditional Greek, Western attitude of man as a detached, objective observer who looks upon nature as an alien and mechanical object to be manipulated and conquered, has been strongly challenged in this age. Parallel with this ecological concern has been the growing interest of many in Eastern religions, such as Taoism and Buddhism, in which man is seen as living in harmony with nature and displaying a reverence for all living creatures in the natural world.[13]

One final observation about the attractiveness of process thought for Christian apologists should be made at this point. Many lines of thought seem to be converging at this time to view life in more holistic, comprehensive terms. Economics, politics, ecology, and religion all seem to demand a global perspective if mankind is to survive. This implies the necessity of a perspective in time which looks much further into the future than most people are willing to accept, and a view of space (territorial relationship) which is much broader and more inclusive than most persons care to admit. Man is forced to acknowledge the interdependence and the interfusion of life with life all over the planet. This has created a greater interest among some Christians to understand other religious perspectives. Some theologians, for instance, view process philosophy as a way of breaking down the walls which have so long separated Protestantism and Roman Catholicism.[14]

The great source of inspiration for the process view on the side of Catholicism has come from a

Jesuit Priest by the name of Teilhard de Chardin (1881-1955). Teilhard was a distinguished French scientist (a paleontologist) whose view of life had been greatly influenced both by Darwin's theory of evolution and the French philosopher Henri Bergson's concept of process as the essential nature of man. (Bergson's thought, also, had a great influence on the development of Whitehead's philosophy.15)

It was Teilhard's genius to bring together a magnificent vision of the entire process of reality, as seen through the eyes of a scientist, with a mystical religious understanding of the _telos_ (the end, or purpose) of creation. He was convinced that modern science opened up the great mysteries of the universe to man, from the intricacies of the atom to the incomprehensible vastness of the galaxies, which could make man ever more aware of the great power and purpose of God. He believed that the mysterious power of the universe was drawing all things into higher and higher levels of complexity, awareness, and self-consciousness. In his book, The Divine Milieu, Teilhard tries to break down artificial barriers between science and religion, life in the material world and life as a Christian. Matter and spirit are not separate entities but belong together. Indeed, spiritual energy permeates the whole of the universe and is capable of making divine all human endeavors. His most significant theological work, The Phenomenon of Man, conbined his faith in evolutionary progress with his faith in Christ. The _telos_ of mankind evolving is the "Omega" point--the point at which all lines of evolution converge and take on their maximum meaning and spirituality. The goal of all processes in the cosmos is the "Center" of all centers, the power within and through all matter--God (Love).16

Since all theology must begin with the notion of God, what is it that process theologians see as a distinct advantage to the use of process philosophy over more classical philosophy as a basis for thinking about God? In traditional theism God is wholly transcendent, above, beyond, and prior to the world of men; He is wholly a self-contained Being and totally abstract, impassive, unchangeable, and all perfection; He is absolute, eternal, all powerful, Creator, giver of all laws and all values, source of all knowledge and all truth. God is known otherwise only through Special Revelation. Process philosophy allows God not only these functions of His "primordial" nature, which place no limitations upon Him, but it, also, allows for immanent, relational, concrete, participant, limited, "consequent" characteristics, which make God's immanence important. For the most part process theologians have been "panentheistic" in their view of God. This means that they have tried to select a course which avoids two extremes in thinking about the nature of God. The one extreme is that of the God of deism, which asserts that God is totally unrelated to and completely transcends his creation, the other extreme is pantheism, which declares that God is nature and is identified as everything in the concrete world.

There are a number of theologians today who have contributed much to the use of process thought as a philosophical base for doing Christian theology. Certainly one of the most distinguished is the late Daniel Day Williams (1910-1973), Roosevelt Professor of Systematic Theology at Union Theological Seminary, in New York City, and formerly on the faculties of Chicago Theological Seminary, and the Federated Theological Faculty of the University of Chicago. Perhaps his most significant book for process thought is The Spirit and the Forms of Love (1968) in which he interprets the Christian doctrine of love (agape) on the basis of a God who is involved in a world which is becoming and whose love, therefore, takes new forms in history. Another first generation process theologian, W. Norman Pittenger, should be mentioned as one who has done much over the last three decades to popularize this approach to theology. He served for over thirty years on the faculty of General Seminary, in New York City, after which he moved to England and became a member of the Faculty of Divinity, Cambridge University. In his numerous books he has endeavored to apply process philosophy to various Christian doctrines. His book, The Word Incarnate (1959), is an extended examination of the work and person of Jesus in the light of process thought.[17] His little book Process Thought and Christian Faith (1968) is a very good introduction for the general reader. Schubert M. Ogden, professor of Theology at Perkins School of Theology, Southern Methodist University, Dallas, Texas, has in his work The Reality of God and Other Essays (1966) attempted to demonstrate the necessity of God's reality on the basis that he gives meaning to man's life. He, along with John B. Cobb, Jr.

make up the most significant advocates of process theology at the present.

COBB

Cobb, an ordained Methodist minister, is probably the most systematic theologian of all the process theologians. In his book, <u>A Christian Natural Theology: Based on the Thought of Alfred North Whitehead</u> (1965),[18] Cobb declares that Whitehead's philosophy ranks along with Plato's, Aristotle's, and Kant's as one of the most creative philosophies of all times. And that because of Whitehead's excellence as a philosopher, and because Cobb is convinced that Whitehead has a "Christian" vision of reality, he has selected his philosophy as the only suitable basis for a Christian natural theology.[19] Cobb, the son of Christian missionaries, was born in Kobe, Japan, in 1925. He was educated at Emory University, Atlanta, Georgia, and took his Ph.D. at the Divinity School of the University of Chicago in 1952, where he studied philosophy under Charles Hartshorne. It was from Hartshorne that Cobb developed his understanding and love of the philosophy of Whitehead. Cobb has taught at Young Harris College, Georgia, Emory University, and is presently Ingraham Professor of Theology at the Southern California School of Theology, Claremont, California. He is the author of numerous books and articles, the co-editor of a technical journal called <u>Process Studies</u>, and a frequent lecturer. In 1965-66 he was a Fulbright Visiting Professor at Johannes Gutenberg University in Mainz, Germany.

His Theological Method

A few comments must be made about Cobb's theological method before looking at his treatment of several specific theological issues.

Cobb chooses to follow Paul Tillich by using the terms "ultimate concern" and "faith" interchangeably. He defines "theology" in a very broad sense as a coherent statement of faith (or expression of one's ultimate concern) about matters which are controlled by the vision of reality as shared by a given community.[20] He notes that definitions should not be considered as either true or false but by the degree of their helpfulness. This definition is helpful, he contends, because it rules out a mere objective ap-

proach to religion (such as that employed in the sociology of religion); it does not restrict the subject matter of theology sharply; it makes no reference to the term "God." Cobb notes that this last
point may appear strange since the root meaning of
the term "theology" is reasoning about God. However, its advantages are the recognition of much
theological work which does not treat the topic of
God, and the fact that it makes possible to include
the thinking found in some forms of Buddhism which
consider the topic of God only in terms of his non-
existence. This definition would allow for the speaking of "Buddhist theology" in reference to that
thought which arises out of the Buddhist community.[21]

Cobb indicates two additional advantages to his
definition of theology. It makes no reference to
the "sacred" or the holy. To define theology as
having to do primarily with the sacred would rule
out the work of many who consider themselves theologians, but whose basic concerns are with doctrines
dealing with the meaning of life which are usually
considered secular, e.g., communism, fascism, romantic
naturalism, and humanism. Under Cobb's definition
these viewpoints must be considered "theology" because they are expressive of a vision of reality, an
ultimate concern or faith, formed in a community. The
final feature of this definition is that it excludes
from theology the activity of the originator of the
community. Such a person may be a genius but not
necessarily a theologian. Again, Cobb would stress
that the usefulness of his definition, since it is so
inclusive, is a matter of degree. This is not to
say that other definitions of theology are unjusti-
fied, it merely recognizes that they draw the lines
of inclusion and exclusion differently.

Now consider the reasons for this very inclusive
definition of theology given by Cobb. He notes that
"natural theology" is often defined as that which man
can discover about ultimate reality on the basis of
reason along. Reason, in this context, is understood
to be a universal power within man which enables him
to gain knowledge of God by his own rational efforts.
Such a definition of "natural theology" has prevailed
in Protestant circles, but has been rejected by more
orthodox Protestants as arrogant and self-deceptive.
How, they ask, can finite man uncover the truths of
the infinite God simply by his own puny reasoning

powers? Nevertheless, this natural theology position has always created some tensions among Protestant thinkers because it has led to the God of the philosophers who is impassive, unchangeable, and Super-transcendent. But the God revealed in the Bible is involved in and with His creation. He is seen as a suffering, compassionate, loving God. Cobb's concern is to rescue "natural theology" from its identification with the above kind of classical philosophy.

Cobb contends that there is no principle inherent in reason which demands that philosophy must always end up with a "god" who is wholly transcendent, immutable, impassive, and unrelated to the world of men. Indeed, process philosophy is a notable demonstration that this is not the case.[22] He also contends that "natural theology" does not establish final conclusions merely on the grounds of rational procedures but that such conclusions must fit coherently into a vision of reality, or an intuited ultimate concern. Cobb acknowledges that every argument begins with premises which in themselves cannot be proved. Such premises become articles of faith.

At the same time, Cobb points out that the "dogmatic" theologians (those who claim to start solely with special revelation) can not avoid philosophical assumptions.[23] The dogmatic theologian must either become more and more unreasonable and authoritative in his theology, or acknowledge the necessity of something like natural theology in his work. This means that the theologian must either choose a philosophy which is adaptable and compatible with his vision of reality (or faith), or he must create his own philosophy. The latter alternative is very unlikely which means that the theologian really has but one choice--to adapt and adopt someone elses philosophy. Cobb suggests two guidelines for doing this. First, the theologian should consider the superiority of the structure of thought he wishes to assimilate. Second, there is no reason to adopt a philosophy that is hostile to the vision of reality held by the Christian community. The intrinsic compatibility and excellence of the philosophy should be of major concern. It should share the fundamental vision of reality as that held by the Christian community. That portion of the philosophy which then deals most relevantly with the Christian faith (questions about God, the

Christ, man, salvation) becomes the theologian's
"Christian natural theology."[24]

It should now be apparent that for Cobb "natural
theology" is necessary. It is the conscious, critical
recognition of the overlapping functions of philosophy and theology. Christian natural theology embodies
thinking that has been done and judged on the basis
of philosophical criteria, but it embodies, also, the
particular concerns and perspective derived from the
Christian community. Since Cobb is convinced that
Whitehead's philosophy is deeply affected by the Christian vision of reality, at least in its starting point,
he appropriates process philosophy as an appeal to the
general evidence available to man both outside the
Christian community and within the community as vindi-
cation of the faith.[25]

God and the World

In the "Preface" of his book God and the World,
Cobb declares that it is a false notion to think that
we may choose either God or the world.[26] Rather, God
is in the world and the world is in and from God. We
cannot pit one against the other for to do so is really
to reject both! Devotion to a God who is not interrelated with the world is a rejection of the God known
through Christ. Certainly it would be a rejection of
God as Cobb interprets the thought of Whitehead.[27]
Cobb's doctrine of "panentheism" endeavors to salvage
the positive concerns of both theism and pantheism
with respect to the relationship of God to space.
Cobb contends that the primary concern of traditional
theism is not the spatial separateness of God and the
world, but that God has integrity in himself and that
he is not some impersonal Whole. Theism denies that
man is a subordinated part of that whole lacking in
individual integrity. Pantheism, on the other hand,
is a protest against an external manipulator, according to Cobb. It is a rejection of a God who operates
from outside of and over against the world. It asserts that God permeates the world and is apparent in
all its aspects.[28] Panentheism has provided a way,
conceptually, to preserve both transcendence and immanence in thinking about God's relationship to the
world. It embraces the notion of God's independence

("primordial nature") and his interdependence ("consequent nature"), or his affecting and affected nature, with respect to reality.

The Argument for God's Existence

Before examining the characteristics of God as primordial and consequent, what, briefly, is the nature of Whitehead's argument for God's existence? Has his conceptualization "proved" the existence of God? If not, what value has his argument? These are the questions raised by the philosopher. As to the question of "proof," Cobb readily admits that there is no inescapable certain proof that will lead one to believe in God's existence on the basis of reason alone. However, the value of the argument, as was indicated earlier, depends upon the appropriateness of the picture given about the general character of the observable (and non-observable) universe and the intuited vision of reality. As Whitehead pointed out a proof rests upon the self-evidence of its premises.[29] The nature of Whitehead's argument for God's existence is essentially a descriptive one. It is the traditional cosmological argument based upon the order of things as seen or known to a ground of order. If the descriptive explanation is sufficiently persuasive and accepted, then certain conclusions appear necessary.

Cobb points out that there is a strong intuition among people that the orderliness of nature and the world demands some explanation that cannot be attributed solely to those things in themselves. There appears to be some other force at work in the universe giving it direction, or coded messages, besides random variation. The movement of nature toward more intricate, complex, and dynamic forms or order, which become more delicate to sustain, but more valuable for life, demand an explanation.[30]

The great significance of Whitehead's analysis of the phenomena of life, nature, and its structures, lies in its thoroughness and adequacy of description which led him to a doctrine of God as the ground and source of order in the cosmos. According to Cobb, Whitehead was led to the notion of God almost in spite of himself.[31] However, even more important than the fact that Whitehead could not understand the world apart from God, is that he viewed it in organic terms.

80

The Principle of Limitation

Cobb contends that Whitehead's first use of the
concept of "God" resulted from his discovery that
actual individual entities, or things, could not exist
unless there was a given aim or goal for them. But
this "giveness" or aim presupposes some order of values
or limitations. Such a principle of limitation, or
ordering of values, Whitehead initially attributed
to God.[32] In his later writings Whitehead became
clearer as to the function of this principle of limitation. He identifies the principle as "primordial,"
and, thereby, clearly indicates that it is God's time-
less, unchanging, eternal envisagement of possibilities
for all entities. Secondly, the primordial specifies
the initial telos for each new occasion of events.[33]
In other words, God's primordial nature is wholly unaffected by time and processes, but it embraces the
vision for ideal fulfillment of each and every possible entity in time and space, and specifies the
initial purpose of each entity.

The philosophical question at this point is
"How does this abstract principle or notion of God's
primordial nature affect the universe? How does God
actualize himself in time and space?" As has been
indicated already in this chapter, Whitehead was convinced of the continuity, the unity, the interrelated-
ness, the dynamic organic-like character of all reality. Reality is in process! This being the case man
may come to understand the processes of reality most
clearly by a rational, critical examination of human
experience.[34] The only hopeful model for understanding the mystery of reality, or the mode of divine being,
is human experience as such. Just as in the human experience there is both a mental (subjective) and physical (objective) pole which share in the apprehension
of the world, so, analogously speaking, within the
nature of God there must be something crudely similar
to a mental (primordial) and physical (consequent,
affecting and affected) embodiment of reality. However, the force of this analogy can only be appreciated
when it is recognized that mental apprehensions actually take precedence over physical or sensory awareness. Whitehead's technical philosophy takes great
pains to establish the priority of the mental opera-
tion in the transformation of received stimuli in
the human environment.[35] But neither the mental pole
nor the physical pole can give a complete explanation

of human experience. Human experience, and all actual
entities, are unities which are composed of a series
of syntheses of both poles. Consequently, the principle of continuity in Whitehead's thought demands a
temporal or physical pole for the completion of God's
nature. This becomes God's consequent nature, that
is, the agent of creation and creativity, the objectification of reality, the point of interaction for God
and the world.

It is at this point that professor Cobb becomes
somewhat distressed with Whitehead for the lack of
rigor in the application of his own principles to the
doctrine of God. A deficiency which Cobb endeavors to
remedy by taking a more "coherent" approach to process
philosophy than did its originator.[36] Cobb asserts
that Whitehead frequently gives the impression that
God is simply the addition of his primordial and consequent natures, and that the consequent nature is
more a matter of speculation than an extension which
is essential in Whitehead's metaphysics. He points
out that Whitehead's own principles assert that actual
things are unities which combine the mental and physical poles of such entities. It is only the actual
entity that acts and not merely one or the other of
its poles. At the same time one pole or another may
be more dominant in any one of its functions. Certainly Whitehead meant to say as much about the two
functions of God's nature.

God's Primordial and Consequent Natures

Cobb's doctrine of God declares that the actual
events that occur in time are a unique synthesis of
both God's primordial and consequent natures.[37] God's
primordial nature provides the aim or ideal for the
self-actualization of each occasion and its manifestation in time derives from God's consequent nature
combined with the affect the past and the present
may have upon it.[38] While God is always the reason
that each new entity becomes, what that entity
(thing or person) becomes is always a combination of
things from the past, the present, and God. The principle of the interdependence of all things applies
even to God. God gives himself to the world, influences its direction and progress, but the world
also gives itself back to him making him responsive
to all that takes place in the world whether it be
its suffering or joy. God in his consequent nature

82

is the guarantee that all process in the universe
will ultimately be progress. The values of the present are woven into the values of the past and together they will create new values for the future and
be transformed into a new unity by God. To serve God
is to conserve and promote the highest values of his
creation. A concern for God apart from a concern for
the world and its creations is faithlessness!

God, according to Cobb, envisages and orders all
pure possibilities.[39] This means that God's ideal
for every actual occasion is present or felt with the
actualization of every such occasion, but alternative
influences of lesser relevance to this ideal are also
present. Even though the novel occasion may not
actualize that which God envisioned for it, it will
include no possibilities which were not provided by
him in his initial envisagement as having some relevance for it. God is the source of all potential possibilities.

Panentheism

Cobb's interpretation of how God is related to
the world in space and time is (as was indicated above
in the discussion of panentheism) very important for
his thought. In man's cosmic experience space and
time together constitute an extensive continuum. Ours
is a spatiotemporal universe. So the question of the
philosopher is whether the fact that man occupies
spatiotemporal regions means that God, likewise, must
occupy time and spatial regions. Whitehead's metaphysics equally allowed for God to be nonspatial or
omnispatial, according to Cobb. Therefore, Cobb declares that an omnispatial God makes more sense because he believes that it brings a greater coherence
to the metaphysical system.[40] His basic criterion
here is that that doctrine of God which is always pre-
ferrable is the one which, other things being equal,
interprets God as more like other entities in terms
of relationships rather than less. The adoption of
this principle implies that God, like all actual entities, has a standpoint. However, such a standpoint
could not possibly favor any one region over any other
region of the universe and, therefore, must be equally
related to all regions. Such an "all-inclusive" relationship, on the part of God, makes it possible for
Cobb to assert that God is physically present to the
world.[41] Which means that God's standpoint includes

all other contemporary standpoints. While God and all
entities interact as separate entities, he includes the
standpoints of every entity within his own standpoint.

Cobb endeavors to explain this view of God in
less technical terms by his description of God as
"energy-events."[42] The physical scientists declare
that the solid objects and other forms of matter which
make up the universe are really all different stages
of energy. The solid table upon which lie a stack of
books is actually composed of subatomic particles, such
as neutrons, protons, and electrons, which are in
rapid motion acting and reacting against one another.
Hence that object in the environment which may be
thought of as being most static, solid, and physical
has an inwardness (a "subjectivity") to it which is
not at all apparent. That which appears most un-
changable and constant, such as a slab of marble,
from the outside is really inside a succession of
happenings among electrons interacting with each
other gradually changing its form. The physicist
declares that these invisible subatomic particles are
the building blocks of the universe which are really
all reducible to one thing - energy.

Cobb asserts that this reduction of physical
things to energy-events should help overcome the common
notion that those things in the world which are most
real are physical or tangible. He believes that it
would be more accurate to recognize the importance
of the inwardness or "subjectivity" of things, especially when dealing with the organic. Man is a combination of energy-events--those outside his body
and those within his brain. The relationship of mind
to matter must deal with the complex energy-events of
consciousness and thinking and their interaction with
more elementary energy-events which display neither
of these two characteristics. The act of thinking
is, itself, the result of past and present energy-
events. Thinking cannot be reduced to the mere activity of physical stimuli as the behavioral scientists
contend. The act of thinking has its own unique
unity and novelty, however, it should not be considered as something which belongs to an entirely
different order of being.

Cobb contends that it is possible to perceive
the notion of energy-events as capable of embracing
both the level of unconscious electronic events and

the activities of man's thinking and that this procedure can be extended to conceptualizations of God.
When man becomes aware of the invisible, or nonsensory power (the electronic event) that operates throughout the universe and even within the very brain cells
of the mind, he is much more responsive to the concept of spirituality. While there are distinct differences between the energy-events of an electron and
the energy-events of mental processes, it is possible
to imagine a similar process of energy-events taking
place between man and God. If such events, despite
the great diversity of their character, represent
what is most real about the inorganic as well as the
organic, then God can be thought of as the ultimate
energy-event.

The common characteristic of all energy-events
is that they are in process and thus express a great
diversity in the degree of change and novelty depending upon where they fall "up" and "down" the scale
in the continuum of matter. To think of a divine
energy-event as a conscious "subject" (inwardness)
which shares in the whole continuum of reality makes
possible the idea of an omnispatial or all-inclusive
standpoint. But before this understanding of God
can be made completely clear, Cobb believes that it
is necessary to examine more closely the human experience.

The Person as an Analogy

It is Cobb's contention that God must be perceived of more in terms of a "living person" rather
than as merely an actual entity, which is the position Whitehead took.[43] While Cobb has indicated the
way in which God may be related to the world spati-
ally, what about his relationship in time? All
things, other than God, are temporal and perish in
physical time. God in his primordial nature (the
mental pole) is above time or is eternal. However,
God in his consequent nature (the physical pole)
is involved in process. He is everlastingly growing
which ultimately means progress in time. Temporal
occasions are real for God. He is affected by them
and he, in turn affects them. But there is no loss
in God of what is past, as in the case of man, or
lack of self-identity through time. Whatever enters
into God as consequent nature remains there forever

with no loss, however new elements are continuously added. God as consequent nature is affected by time and affects time but conserves all the values of time.

Again, Cobb states that he must insist upon the indissoluble unity of the two natures of God and that the best model for this is that of the human person. As a living person man is affected by and affects his physical continuum at any given moment in time, as a succession of experiences, but through his mental life, memory makes it possible for him to rise above the temporal experience and to perceive of himself as a unity, a whole, and to conserve his greatest values. Man remembers his past and looks forward to his future and in so doing retains his personal identity. God at any given moment is an actual entity affected by and affecting the world, but, like man, satisfaction is attained by him through the successive phases of his becoming.

Again, the subjective experience of man is the closest analogue for thinking of God's relationship to the world in time even though the analogy is not actually very close. To be specific, man's subjective experiences are highly dependent upon sensory experiences whereas there is no reason to believe that such would be the case with God. Cobb points out that a similar analogy must be drawn with respect to the subjectivity of the electron and human experience.[44] To avoid the old dualisms of subjects and objects Cobb declares (following Whitehead) that man must realize that events which occur in this very moment are subjective (usually of an unconscious nature) which then pass into an objective event and become the phenomena for new subjects. The phenomena of energy-events derived from the electron when grouped into large societies appear to man's sense organs as something physical. However, Cobb declares that human experience is not basically sensory if what is meant by that entails hearing, seeing, and touching. Man does not hear, see or touch the electron and yet it is the basis of all energy. Electronic events must, like man, have something analogous to subjectivity.

Just as it was necessary to get behind what is commonly believed to be the physical in order to understand the subjective power of the universe, Cobb asserts it is necessary to get behind what is commonly believed to be the basic "givens" of human experience in order to understand the way in which God operates in the universe. The energy-event in which the table image arises in man's mind is the result of a highly complex chain of organized impressions and apprehensions. It is fundamentally a mental image which occurs somewhere in the region of a man's brain. The most immediate cause of the image results from subcellular events in the mind which by a complex process of recall and organization of past experiences leads to those momentary impressions which bombarded the eye. "This means that the fundamental data for the human mind or subject are not physical objects outside the body, but energy-events within the body."[45]

Cobb believes that this understanding of the subjective side of human nature helps to understand what nonsensory experience is. While man does not doubt the reality of past and future, neither are open to direct sensory proof. Similarly, man's conviction that there is a real world out there which exists quite independently of human experience is not provable. Man's sense experience as such gives him nothing but particles of sensory impressions in the immediate moment. These nonsensory elements of the human experience are generally below the threshold of consciousness and, consequently, are difficult to focus upon sharply. But, according to Cobb, such nonsensory experiences are the only clues for man of the subjective character of energy-events such as electrons.

When endeavoring to find some analogy that will apply to the subjective nature of God, electrons will hardly suffice. Rather, Cobb believes that we must suppose that those nonsensory experiences in man which are generally obscure and below the threshold of man's consciousness would be fully conscious in God's being. So the best analogy for relating God to the temporal may be in terms of the nonsensory experience of memory. Man may have a very vivid memory of some event which took place in the past. The memory may be so clear that his recall of it may be the equivalent of re-living the experience. But this immediate experience is based upon another occasion which is apprehended in a nonsensory manner.

God - the All-inclusive Standpoint

Cobb has taken the position that God occupies an all-inclusive (omnispatial) standpoint and that the major objection to this view is the belief that two things cannot occupy the same space during the same time. However, as Cobb has tried to show by his analogy of the electron and human subjectivity this is not the case. All entities are a subject of experience as well as an object to be experienced by other subjects. When man's subjective experience is considered (that experience which he perceives most immediately) it obviously has a spatiotemporal standpoint to it. It extends out around him to a considerable degree, embracing an indefinite region of his environment, but it also reaches back into his past and brings into being a new synthesis of inherited data in that particular moment and place. And there is no reason to believe that the electrons which pulsate within his brain at that moment do not "enjoy" an analogous subjectivity of their own within their own limited regions. Still each subjectivity, that of the man and that of the electron, has its own self-identity standpoint independent of the other and yet each influences the other as each passes into objectivity. The energy-events of the brain influences some of the thoughts and feelings of the man while at the same time these thoughts and feelings influence some of the energy transfers of the brain. Consequently, within the same spatiotemporal region there takes place an interchange of energy-events, yet each subjectivity retains its individuality and autonomy as well as its interdependence.[46]

Cobb contends that it is the above mentioned analogy which offers the best understanding of God and the world. God is everywhere, but he is not everything. He is a very special kind of energy-event. He is related to temporal events and especially to the occasions of man's experience as the provider of the ideal for the self-actualization of each occasion. It is in relation to that creative source of all pure possibilities that each human energy-event takes place. God, for the Christian says Cobb, is the "call forward" to ever-greater experiences of love, life, and freedom. He is the "One Who Calls" man to go beyond the accomplishments of the past and the security of tradition to the realization of ever more inclusive values.[47]

The Problem of Evil

Any doctrine of God demands some explanation of
the pain, suffering, and evil experienced by man.
As a doctrine Theism is the belief in an all-powerful and perfectly good being who is the source and
creator of all things. The question that naturally
arises for the Theist is "Why does the author of perfect goodness who is the source of all power allow
his creation to suffer so much evil?" Why is there
so much pain, corruption, and injustice in a world
in which a good and all-powerful God is supposedly in
control?

Cobb believes that the key to the solution of the
problem of evil is to be found, first of all, in a
re-interpretation of the concept of power. Too often
God's power has been understood as compulsion or co-
ercion. But the power that really counts, says Cobb,
is that which persuades. Indeed, it is only by "persuasion" that real power is exercised.[48] It is by
persuasion that even the powerful are persuaded. This
is the manner in which the New Testament expresses
the power of God. It is the kind of influence exercised by a good and wise parent and not that of a ter-
rifying dictator. This means that while God is responsible for the good he is not responsible for the
evil in the world.

A second necessity to arrive at some solution
to the problem of evil is to re-interpret the traditional notion of Biblical theists that God created the
world out of nothing. This notion, along with the
idea that the world was given a fixed form and an un-
alterable goal at the moment of creation, once held
by theologians, does not fit the evolutionary, process
conception of reality. Cobb insists that the only
meaningful way to think of God as creator is to combine
the notion of God as a persuader with the recognition
that God must work with and upon the world given to
him at any given moment.[49] The old view of creation
makes it impossible to explain why God would have
willed into being a creation that is so unaffected
by the resistant to his desire for goodness.

The evolutionary, process concept of reality
makes it possible to interpret the rise of life and
values in the world without maligning God. It is

God who has drawn the world into higher and higher
forms of creativity. With the appearance of organic
life on this planet a new species began to emerge
which produced increasingly higher forms of value.
The appearance of life made possible much more rapid
evolutionary processes, with a much greater variety
of possibilities, which in turn led to greater richness of subjectivity and experience. With the emergence of consciousness, self-consciousness, freedom,
and reason the world entered a new epoch of values.
This whole process can be much better understood as
the call to greater self-actualization. Natural dis-
asters, such as earthquakes and volcanoes, occur only
because life is involved. The violent activity of
matter on some distant star is not considered evil
because man does not perceive of it as destroying some
established value. Despite occasional natural ca-
lamities there is far more richness and value in a
world teeming with life than one in which everything
remains at the inorganic level. Indeed, the very
struggle for existence is a part of the pattern where-by
greater self-actualization is brought into being.

God, then, according to Cobb, must be understood
as that power at work in the world persuading every
entity to maximize itself along the lines of order
and satisfaction.[50] This means that God values immediate satisfaction of entities even at the risk
of orderliness. With the appearance of man the
greatest possibilities for the actualization of values
as well as the destruction of such comes into being.
One of the causes of much evil in the world, according
to Cobb, is due to the incapacity of sub-human species
to be motivated by inclusive objectives. Man is the
only species who has developed this capacity or potentiality for a global or unlimited concern for others
and his world. With man a qualitative distinction
must be made with respect to both his responsibility
for evil and for good. Cobb asserts that "sin"
is the result of man's capacity to corrupt his potentiality for the good. God by creating the ideal of
the good provides the situation for evil.

The third consideration which Cobb insists is
necessary for an adequate re-interpretation of the
problem of evil depends upon a circular kind of affirmation.[51] Cobb has defined God in terms of that being
which calls life and man into self-actualization.

Therefore, the possibility of loving God depends upon the feasibility of affirming the goodness of life and man in spite of the problems of evil. It is not possible to love the creator without loving his creation. But it is equally true that man cannot believe in God without affirming life and humanity, because their goodness is dependent upon the goodness of God.

In the act of faith the Christian accepts God as the embodiment of all those perfections of goodness for which he searches himself and others in vain. The Christian loves God, according to Cobb, for what God is in himself. Despite the terrors which life may hold for him, the Christian affirms God's love in the hope that the future will vindicate his faith. Belief in God sustains the hope in man that the past is not completely lost, and that there is a cumulative character to all his values. It also sustains the hope that perhaps all human experiences are preserved in the divine memory. Belief in God most of all asserts that there is a power for goodness which is operative in the world which lies beyond human frality. Belief in God, finally, entitles man to hope for life after death.

So for Cobb if a man has faith in God he can live with hope. And if he has hope, he can affirm the goodness of life and humanity. And if man can affirm the goodness of life and humanity he can solve existentially the problem of evil, even though he may have to live with the perplexities of some of its questions.[52]

The Progression of Humankind

Cobb's basic optimism about man and the human situation is seen more clearly in his book The Structure of Christian Existence.[53] In this work he sets forth his doctrine of human experience in terms of the categories of historical evolution as seen from a subjective Christian standpoint. It is his endeavor to portray the manner in which man has successively responded to the call forward, since passing into conscious experience, with particular attention given to the Christian claim to uniqueness and finality. Cobb employs the expression "structure of existence" to indicate the range of possibilities for self-understanding and development which man acquires with the crossing of each new threshold of evolution.[54]

Cobb identifies three major thresholds of man's evolution. The first is that unidentifiable point in time when man's ancestors developed a sufficient surplus of psychic energy to seek satisfaction which did not serve the functional needs of the body. Rather, the psychic life became an end in itself, unconsciously of course, rather than primarily a tool for the promotion of health and survival. But the whole process of the psychic activity rested upon symbolization (language being its major forms). While man retained his continuity with his ancestory by responding to signals, a basic ability found in all animals of intelligence, symbolization was primary. Symbolization arose in the unconscious mind whereas intelligent perception and response arose out of receptive consciousness. It was in the unconscious, symbolic psyche of man that a vast autonomous development took place leading to the "reflective consciousness" which became the distinguishing attribute of man.[55]

The second threshold of progress was the development of a "civilization" in which cities were built.[56] Cobb identifies this stage of human development as emerging for the first time in the fourth millennium before Christ. Its distinguishing characteristic is that man begins the process of the rationalization of his reflective consciousness. The kind of rationality which Cobb has in mind here is not a highly developed type of logical deduction or induction. Rather, it is merely the unconscious awareness of contradiction. Mythical mentality, he asserts, is not bothered by contradictions. Man at this new stage of his development made use of his symbols, and not merely signals, to interpret and organize his environment.

Individuality and Freedom

The third major threshold across which mankind has moved is the continued rationalization of reflective consciousness. Following the lead of Karl Jaspers, Cobb calls this epoch of human evolution the "axial period." However, Cobb expands upon Jaspers' interpretation of this period in terms of its diversity, successive stages, and by adding Christianity as a further threshold not accounted for by Jaspers.[57] The distinguishing mark of axial man is the new role which rationality played in his life. In principle, the conscious control was extended to all areas of man's action and thought. This was the result of man's continued reflection upon his conscious symbols. This meant that man became increasingly estranged from the mythical world in which his ancestors had lived until, finally, there appeared those men who had the rational perspective to destroy the power of the mythical world altogether. It was this radical break with the mythical age which characterizes the axial period.

According to Cobb, the crossing of this threshold is illustrated by the gradual development within man of individuality and freedom.[58] The epoch of civilized man provided the necessary conditions within which axial man could gradually develop a new concept of himself as a free individual. However, a new category of conceptualization is needed to understand man at this stage of the evolutionary process. Cobb designates this new category as the "seat of existence."[59] It indicates that even though much of man's psychic life remained unconscious, with its own centers of organization which were unknown to the consciousness, it gained a new unity of its own. This new unity developed around some determining point of view or perspective--such as that of Socratic man who identified himself with reason, or that of prophetic (Hebrew) man who identified himself with a center transcending passion and reason alike.

In keeping with his process view of philosophy, Cobb does not want to give the impression that each of the successive epochs of man's evolution, as primitive, civilized, and axial, constitute a single type of man. There were variations among and within the several stages of development which shaded off into each other. There is always some continuity, as well as some new elements, present in the evolutionary process. However, the range of diversity is much greater among axial man than what would be found between primitive man and civilized man. Cobb elaborates five kinds of axial existence: Buddhist, Homeric, Socratic, Prophetic, and Christian. While the "seat of existence" in all axial men is located in rational consciousness, each representative group has endeavored to go beyond the structure of existence given to it as axial man. However, it is only in Christianity, says Cobb, that a new threshold is crossed in the further development of man.

Spiritual Existence - A New Conception

The new seat of existence, "spiritual existence," is dependent upon a radically different conceptualization of responsibility and love. This new conception of man came about as the result of the message of Jesus and the experience of the primitive post resurrection Christian church.[60] Cobb points out that the most immediate predecessor of spiritual existence is that of prophetic (Hebrew) existence or "personal" existence. Personal existence is that structure of existence which developed within prophetic Judaism in which the conscious psyche transcended passion and reason as impersonal forces. Personal existence emerged out of the prophetic tradition of such men as Jeremiah. It was the results of a development in which man assumed that he had been individually confronted by, or commanded by, God, and thereby placed in a position of having to make a conscious, inward decision. It is that self-conscious individuality, which rises above impersonal emotions and reason, which Cobb asserts justifies the concept of "person."[61] In personal existence the person, the "I," becomes the agent for controlling its own thoughts and feelings. However, the "I" cannot be responsible for its own limitations, for that which lies beyond its own power.

Spiritual existence introduces man to an extremely more radical concept of responsibility. The basic command of God deals precisely with those aspects of the self, the "I," overwhich the self has no control. Spiritual existence was, according to Cobb, the consequence of Jesus' message combined with the primitive Christian community's experience of the Holy Spirit which made possible the transcendence of the self as the last barrier to total responsibility. In contrast to personal existence, spiritual existence is responsible for that which lies within its power as well as for that which lies beyond its power. Spiritual existence must accept responsibility for not only what it is but for what it is not! Cobb calls it "radically self-transcending" in terms of the notion of responsibility. Spiritual existence makes possible new depths of sin and corruption for man, as well as new heights of self-sacrificial love and neighbor concern. But radical self-transcendence in terms of human responsibility is, also, absolutely dependent upon a new understanding of love.

94

The seat of existence for prophetic man was the love of God. God was the determining factor of man's life. The essence of Hebrew devotion is to love God and the proof of that love is obedience to God's law. This obedience was right and good because of what God had done for Israel. It was right and good because God was just and merciful and would award man accordingly. Therefore, what was advantageous to the individual was also right and the faithful man knew that he must serve God despite personal inclinations. However, this situation gave rise to the distinct awareness that man may choose to love God either for his own advantage or as an end in itself. The situation also gave rise to man's awareness of his relationship with other persons. If there was a right way and a wrong way to love God, the same situation obviously prevailed in interpersonal relationships. Man could not simply ignore the dangers of his self-centeredness. The deeper reality which had forced man to look at the divine-human relationship, also, forced him to look at the man-man relationship. Hence, the right relationship with the neighbor was to love him for his own sake, as he would naturally love himself, and not for some advantage to the self. However, this commandment to "love your neighbor as yourself" was directed to the "I," to the agent or will of the person. Consequently, such a command was not interpreted as a challenge to self-centeredness but as a directive to the will to do what it was capable of doing. Cobb points out that prophetic man never seriously considered the question whether when a man acts justly he is indeed acting simply for the good of his neighbor, or whether he is motivated for his own righteousness.[62]

The Focus Shifts to Motives

It is only in Christianity and the rise of spiritual existence that man's basic self-centered preoccupation is recognized and dealt with victoriously. The commandments to love God and the neighbor remain central, but their meaning is completely transformed.[63] Love is now recognized as that intention or feeling which gives rise to action and, therefore, as something which naturally comes into conflict with self-centeredness when man is commanded to do something. The focus of attention is now much more upon the heart of man, his motives, rather than his actions as such. It is in the psychic life of man, the inner man, where God's

spirit dwells and acts. Outward acts of obedience
and justice are not enough. Now man is understood as
being responsible, not merely for his outward acts,
but for his innermost motives as well. Now man is
commanded to be perfect even as God is perfect! Yet
try as he may he finds all sorts of resistances to
such commands within his inner life. Indeed, his self-
centeredness becomes a kind of obsession which cuts
him off from healthy openness to others. It becomes
a kind of spiritual pride, or self-preoccupation
which distorts, corrupts, and taints his thoughts and
actions. It becomes a form of spiritual sickness.

The Dilemma

As this point spiritual man faces a dilemma. The
only escape from his spiritual sickness is to love without self-regard. But his every effort to love is a
further expression of his self-regard and only in-
tensifies his problem. Thus, spiritual man's only
salvation is love but it is not attainable by his own
efforts. He must resort to an outside source of power.
Cobb declares that man must discover that he is already
accepted, or knows himself as loved, even in the sickness of his self-preoccupation, before he, in turn,
can love and accept others. It is the experience of
this gift of undeserved love, which frees the "I" from
its self-preoccupation, which makes possible the self-
transcending self of spiritual existence. Therefore,
the Christian claim to finality and uniqueness lies
in this deep consciousness of personal responsibility
and love that is self-transcending which makes possible spiritual existence.

Before bringing to a close this description of
Cobb's natural theology a few observations should be
made with respect to its adequacy. Certainly one of
the greatest apologetic assets of process thought is
its relevance to the ecological crisis of our age.
The interfussion and interdependence of life and
matter, of the individual entity with the whole of
the environment, is the key to finding solutions to
the global problems of mankind. To the extent that
contemporary man becomes aware of this scientific
understanding of life and matter, it would seem that
the process theologian's day has come. A God who is
thought of not only as the source of order in the

universe, but as the Cosmic "persuader," the One who calls man into greater and greater involvement with the creative processes of life in the present and the future, the One who not only influences but is also influenced, might very well revive the faith of man. The optimism about man and his essential role in the actualizations of creative progress in the world, the belief in the power of man's rational ability to solve the insuperable problems of existence, might very well be Cobb's greatest contribution to theology in this age of despair.

However, in the light of such immense global disruptions, hunger, and suffering as this age is witnessing, in the light of the ever-increasing contradictions and ambiguities brought about by scientific technological "progress"--the tool of rational man-- is Cobb's appeal to greater rational coherence and mental abstractions helpful? Critics have often pointed out that Whitehead is an "essentialist." An essentialist is one who believes that the universe exhibits a rational, purposive structure at its very core and that the human mind is capable of understanding and giving expression to this essential nature, if not with complete finality, at least with highly dependable accuracy. Consequently, man's reason, even though finite, is in no way distorted when applied scrupulously to the structures of reality and so is capable of knowing whatever truth can be known about nature, his own being, and even about God. Cobb almost seems to fall into the essentialist camp when he insists that Whitehead did not follow the dictates of his own logic vigorously enough when thinking about God's Primordial and Consequent natures as actual entities and as living person. This enormous assumption that consistent, coherent, critical thought about human experience will present to man realities not directly experienced but affirmed simply because they make man's experience as a whole more orderly, is itself questionable. The cosmological and teleological arguments of the philosophers really prove nothing about the ultimate nature of reality. Cobb recognizes this point but still proceeds to order his whole theological structure around these notions.

Cobb seemingly has little concern for traditional Christian sources or tradition, particularly Biblical sources, when it comes to systematic theology. Perhaps for this reason he has very little to say about the

97

human predicament, its estrangement, its "sin," but chooses, rather, to focus almost exclusively upon spiritual man and future man.[64] Does the minimizing of man's ambiguities, his pride, his self-preoccupation really convince a theistic skeptic of God's reality? Are the perplexities and contradictions of man's experience of evil and tragedy actually made more acceptable to the Christian, or to the theistic skeptic, by giving him a finite God, or by simply redefining the terms? These are some of the questions that appear to be unanswered by Cobb's process theology.

[1]For more autobiographical information see
Alfred N. Whitehead, Essays in Science and Philosophy
(Philosophical Library, Inc., 1947), Part I. Also,
Norman Pittenger, Alfred North Whitehead (John Knox
Press, 1969), pp. 1-10, gives an excellent account
of Whitehead's life, marriage, writings, lectures,
teaching, books, and final years.

[2]See Pittenger, op. cit., pp. 10-12, for a concise account of Hartshorne's life, teaching, writings,
and career.

[3]Whitehead sets forth the demands of "Specula-
tive Philosophy" and defines his terms in Part I of
Process and Reality: An Essay in Cosmology (The Macmillan Company, 1929). An excellent exposition of
his metaphysics can be found in Ivor Leclerc, Whitehead's Metaphysics (The Macmillan Company, 1958).

[4]Whitehead makes this idea especially clear in
his lecture on "Nature Alive" in Modes of Thought
(The Macmillan Company, 1938), Chap. VIII. Cf. the insights of the renowned biologist and ecologist Barry
Commoner, The Closing Circle: Nature, Man, and Technology (Alfred A. Knopf, 1972), ch. 2, especially his
first law of ecology.

[5]A very readable account which sets forth many
of the basic concepts of process thought in non-
technical language is found in Barry Wood's book The
Magnificent Frolic (The Westminster Press, 1970),
ch. 2, entitled "The Seamless Robe of Nature."

[6]See Whitehead, Process and Reality, p. 10f. Cf.,
also, Part II, ch. X.

[7]Ian G. Barbour, Issues in Science and Religion
(Prentice-Hall, Inc., 1966), pp. 344-347, has a very
good discussion of this concept. Cf. also his brief
summary of Process Philosophy pp. 128-131.

[8]Cf. Process and Reality, pp. 521-523.

[9]See ibid., pp. 523 ff.

[10]Cf. ibid., p. 377; cf. Barbour, op. cit., pp.
439-441.

[11]See Norman Pittenger, Process Thought and Christian Faith (Macmillan Company, 1968), pp. 20-22f. Cf.,
also, Barbour, op. cit., p. 454.

[12]Pittenger applies this to "situational" and
"contextual ethics." See Process Thought and Christian Faith, p. 91.

[13]A good example of this kind of developing awareness is presented in a work edited by Ian G. Barbour,
Earth Might Be Fair: Reflections on Ethics, Religion,
and Ecology (Prentice-Hall, Inc., 1972).

[14]Cf. C. J. Curtis, Contemporary Protestant Thought
(The Bruce Publishing Company, 1970), chap. XIV. This
work is one of the volumes in a "Contemporary Theology Series" edited by two Roman Catholics, J. Frank
Devine and Richard W. Rousseau, both members of the
Society of Jesus. Cf., also, Pittenger, Process
Thought and Christian Faith; and Bernard Lee, The Becoming of The Church: A Process Theology of the Structures of Christian Experience (Paulist Press, 1974).

[15]See Daniel Day Williams, The Spirit and the Forms
of Love (Harper and Row, Publishers, 1968), pp. 104-
105.

[16]See Teilhard de Chardin, The Phenomenon of Man
(Harper Torchbooks, 1961), p. 294. There are, of
course, a number of differences between Teilhard and
Whitehead but essentially they compliment one another.
The Whiteheadians, probably, are more devoted to the
abstract cosmological picture, whereas the Teilhardians
seem to put more emphasis upon the spiritual vision
of the progressive divinization (or spiritualization)
of mankind. As Daniel Day Williams points out, the
Teilhardian view of the Omega point is absolute whereas the Whiteheadians seem content to live with an
open-ended process of creativity in the cosmos. See
Williams, "Hope and the Future of Man: A Reflection,"
in Hope and the Future Man, edited by Ewert H. Cousins
(Fortress Press, 1972), pp. 143, 145-146.

[17]Two more recent books which deal with the
problems of Christology from a process perspective
are: David R. Griffin, A Process Christology (The
Westminster Press, 1973); and John B. Cobb, Christ
in a Pluralistic Age (The Westminster Press, 1975).

[18](The Westminster Press, 1965). For a recent
appraisal of Cobb's theological contributions to
process theology see David Ray Griffin and Thomas J.
J. Altizer, eds., John Cobb's Theology in Process
(Westminster Press, 1977).

[19]See op. cit., pp. 16, 268, 269.

[20]See A Christian Natural Theology, pp. 252-270.

[21]See ibid., p. 255.

[22]See ibid., p. 260.

[23]See ibid., pp. 261-263. In his book Living Options in Protestant Theology: A Survey of Methods (The Westminster Press, 1962), Cobb endeavors to make this point clear that all theological positions systematically depend upon assertions that are not inherent to their systems. He notes that Karl Barth comes the closest in avoiding such dependence.

[24]See ibid., p. 266.

[25]See ibid., pp. 268, 280, et passim.

[26]See God and the World (The Westminster Press, 1969), p. 9.

[27]In A Christian Natural Theology, p. 195, Cobb notes that both a nonspatiality and an omnispatiality view of God are equally possible in Whitehead's metaphysics. Therefore, Cobb asserts that we must choose between them on the basis of which is more coherent with the system. Cf., ibid., pp. 194-196, 243-245.

[28]See God and the World, pp. 77-80.

[29]See Modes of Thought, pp. 66-67.

[30]See A Christian Natural Theology, pp. 168-172.

[31]See ibid., p. 173, et passim.

[32]See ibid., pps. 140 ff., for Cobb's very involved discussion of this problem which leaves Whitehead's God as only one of three attributes of ultimate reality.

[33]See ibid., p. 155, et passim.

[34]See The Function of Reason (Princeton University Press, 1929), p. 11; Adventures of Ideas (The Macmillan Company, 1933), pp. 237-245.

[35]See Process and Reality, pp. 163-167. See Cobb's discussion in A Christian Natural Theology, pp. 28-39. Langdon Gilkey calls Whitehead an "essentialist" - see his book review of "A Christian Natural Theology" in Theology Today, XXII (January, 1966), pp. 530-545.

[36]See A Christian Natural Theology, pp. 176 ff.

[37]See ibid., pp. 184-185.

[38]See ibid., pp. 203-214. Cf. God and the World, pp. 81-83.

[39]See A Christian Natural Theology, p. 201.

[40]See ibid., p. 195.

[41]See ibid., p. 196.

[42]See God and the World, pp. 70-80.

[43]See A Christian Natural Theology, pp. 188, 192.

[44]See God and the World, pp. 73-74.

[45]Ibid., p. 74.

[46]See *ibid.*, p. 79.

[47]See *ibid.*, ch. 2, "The One Who Calls."

[48]See *ibid.*, pp. 88-92.

[49]See *ibid.*, pp. 91-92. See also his discussion of the nature of God as creator in A Christian Natural Theology, pp. 203-214. See our discussion above p. 82.

[50]See God and the World, p. 94.

[51]See *ibid.*, pp. 97-102.

[52]Cf. *ibid.*, p. 100.

[53](The Westminster Press, 1967).

[54]See *op. cit.*, pp. 16-17.

[55]See *ibid.*, Chapter Three.

[56]See *ibid.*, Chapter Four.

[57]See *ibid.*, Chapter Five.

[58]See *ibid.*, pp. 55-57.

[59]See *ibid.*, p. 54.

[60]See *ibid.*, Chapter Ten.

[61]See *ibid.*, p. 104.

[62]See *ibid.*, p. 132.

[63]See *ibid.*, Chapter Eleven.

[64]See his article "What Is the Future? A Process Perspective," in Hope and the Future of Man, pp. 1-14, in which he sets forth certain of his own views on eschatology.

CHAPTER FOUR

EXISTENTIAL THEOLOGY

There are a number of ways in which existentialism seems to stand in stark contrast to other philosophies. This is especially true with respect to
process philosophy. Process philosophy is a highly
developed abstract system of thought which begins
with certain scientific observations in nature and
then proceeds to the development of a tightly rea-
soned metaphysical view of the whole. In contrast,
existentialism is a style of philosophizing which at
times appears irrational, subjective, individual, and
not the least interested in developing a complete
"system" of thought. It begins with the inward man
rather than objective nature and concentrates upon
man's existence rather than his status as a thinker.[1]
In contrast to process philosophy existentialism
has a much longer history and has had a great influence upon the thought of men in many walks of life
other than the disciplines of philosophy and theology.
In recent decades its impact upon the literature,
psychology, drama, and the visual arts of the Western
world has been particularly noticeable.[2]

Basic Characteristics

Perhaps the major reason for this broad and significant influence of existentialism is due to certain recurring themes which focus upon the meaning of
personal existence. All the existentialist philosophers endeavor to deal with man as a decision maker,
as free, and, therefore, a responsible being. Man
as a finite, alienated, despairing, guilt-ridden
creature, who must constantly confront his own death,
is a persistent theme. Indeed, some of the most
brilliant analyses of man's emotional life and his
feeling states have been made by the thinkers in this
tradition beginning with Soren Kierkegaard (1813-55)
and including Martin Heidegger (1889-1976) and Jean-
Paul Sartre (1905-   ).[3]

Very briefly the existentialist may be described
negatively as a protestor.[4] He stands in protest
against the mass mentality which accepts, and has con-
structed, neat little "systems" of organizations as

103

being inevitable and certain. He stands in protest against the institutionalized approach to existence whether it be in the form of political, social, and economic notions of success, or the intellectual, scientific organization of truth. The existentialist is keenly aware of the contradictory nature of being. To be is to be in the face of contradictions, absurdities, hopelessness, and helplessness. The human predicament is ambiguous. With man's love there is always the hatred. With his altruism there is always the selfishness. With his truth there is always the falsity. Man's absolutes are always relative.

At the same time the existentialist may be described positively as an affirmer. He affirms man, or being, in his inwardness, his subjectivity, as the only point of real truth. The true reality of being is not discovered out there somewhere by the use of some detached, rational, systematic method. To be is to exist, to stand out from other existing things. Existence is to ask the basic question of being "What does it mean to be?" True knowledge is participation not observation. It is only as an individual that man truly participates in death, in suffering, or life. Existence means to be now--to be fully, intensely, deeply involved. Existence means commitment. It means to be responsible--to be free!

Its Influence Among Theologians

In recent decades existentialism has been the most influential philosophy among theologians. Indeed, the most creative and influential theologians of this century have incorporated a good deal of existential thought into their own theologies. Its influence can be seen in Protestants like Karl Barth, Rudolf Bultmann, and Paul Tillich, and in the Eastern Orthodox theologian Nikolai Berdyaev, and the Roman Catholic Karl Rahner, and the great Jewish mystic Martin Buber. Perhaps the major contributor to this impact of existentialism upon the theological thinker of recent times has been Soren Kierkegaard.[5] Kierkegaard is usually regarded as the father of modern existentialism. A Danish writer, philosopher, and devout Christian, Kierkegaard was little known outside of Scandinavia until the early part of the twentieth century.

104

As a student at the University of Copenhagen in the early part of the nineteenth century Kierkegaard was trained in the philosophy of Georg Wilhelm Friedrich Hegel (1770-1831). Hegel taught that reality is to be found in the Absolute Idea.[6] This Absolute is God. Hegel believed that the world is in a dialectic process and that the Absolute, Nature, and man's mind, or Thought, constitute a dynamic inter- action. God, or the Absolute, is not some entity separate from the world and man, but is more like a complex organism which embraces the whole. Consequent- ly, God's laws or ideas are impressed upon and ex- pressed by Nature which man in turn can read out by his reason or rationality. Man's way of thinking is structured by Nature and he is able to think about Nature in a way dictated by Nature's inherent struc- ture. Thus, in a sense, when man is thinking rational- ly and consistently he is thinking God's thoughts after Him. It is through Thought that man arrives at a true knowledge of the Absolute.

It was against this Hegelian notion--that reason must turn to the abstract realm of forms and ideas, of "essences," in order to find reality--that Kier- kegaard reacted so strongly. According to John Mac- quarrie, "Modern existentialism begins with Kier- kegaard's championing of the concreteness of existence over against what he took to be the essentialism of Hegel."[7] It is largely due to this radical reaction on the part of Kierkegaard to abstract "system" building and rational coherence which has brought about the charges against him of "irrationalism."

In recent decades two outstanding theologians have made extensive use of existentialist thought as an apologetic aid. Paul Tillich (1886-1965) believed that the existentialist analysis of the human situa- tion raised the critical questions which focused upon man's "ultimate concern."[8] The answers to such ques- tions came by the "method of correlation" from beyond man through Christian revelation. It is the task of systematic theology to demonstrate that the symbols used in the Christian message, such as "the Fall," the "Christ," and "God," have new meaning and sig- nificance in the light of existential analysis of the basic structures of being. Even though Tillich followed the lead of some of the existentialist, such as Heidegger, and developed an ontology of being he did not contend that such an ontology (a philosophical construct of the nature of being or reality) proved the existence or the nature of ultimate reality or God. Indeed, he declared that Natural theology has significance for man only if man is asking the basic question about God and if it gives an adequate description of the human situation.[9] It is when man becomes aware of his finitude that he asks the question of God. According to Tillich, man, as finite being surrounded by the possibility of nonbeing, cannot escape the quest for God, or the ultimate source of all being. He cannot escape his ultimate concern. The existentialist analysis makes man acutely aware of this concern.

The second theologian to make extensive use of existentialism is Rudolf Bultmann (1884-1976). Bultmann, a New Testament scholar and pioneer in form criticism (the study of the origins and development of the literary tradition of the Gospels), is not quite as well known in this country as the great systematic theologian and philosopher Paul Tillich. Perhaps one basic reason for this is that Tillich spent the last half of his life in America and did the major portion of all his writing in this country, whereas Bultmann lived his entire life in Germany. Bultmann studied at the universities of Marburg, Tubingin, and Berlin and was professor of New Testament studies at the universities of Breslau, Giessen, and Marburg (1921-1951). After his retirement from teaching in 1951, Bultmann became very much in the center of the great debate which he had initiated by his program of "demythologizing" the New Testament.[10]

"Demythologizing" is the special term which Bultmann selected to designate his unique method of exegesis, or hermeneutics.[11] It is a method of interpretation. It is specifically a method by which to interpret Scripture. To de-mythologize the Christian message is to declare that that message is not bound up with an ancient "world-view" which included an elaborate cosmological and eschatological myth.

The ancient myths speak of the gods and demons as powers or creatures who actually materialize in this world, although they are from another, transcendent, invisible, or spiritual world. The myths express man's conviction that his destiny or meaning rests with these transcendent, mysterious powers who dwell beyond his jurisdiction. Bultmann asserts that this same mythological view is present in the Bible and that it expresses in a crude way Biblical man's faith in a transcendent God. The mythological world-view of the Bible pictures a three-storied universe filled with angels and devils, heaven and hell, and an age of men held in bondage by Satin, sin, and death all hastening toward a cosmic holocaust. It pictures a pre-existent divine Being sent forth by God to rescue man from certain destruction. This divine Being atones for the sins of men by his death, is resurrected, and deprives the demonic forces of their power, and will come again on the clouds of heaven to complete the works of redemption and judgment. All of this is to happen very soon.[12]

Bultmann contends that such a mythological world-view is no longer acceptable to this scientifically oriented age of men and must be rejected. At the same time, he declares that the deeper dimensions, or truths of the myth, must not be lost. The myth makes man aware that he is not master of his own being and that he is dependent upon a power beyond the visible universe which may deliver him from the destructive forces within this visible existence. Therefore, what is important about mythical imagery, according to Bultmann, is not the imagery itself but the understanding which it communicates to man about his own existence.

The appropriate question to ask with regard to the Bible, declares Bultmann, is the question of personal existence.[13] But man can discover the right way to ask the proper questions about human existence only by applying "objective, critical reflection." At this point, says Bultmann, the interpreter must turn to that philosophy which is most adequate in guiding man into asking the proper questions about human existence. The proper philosophy for Bultmann is Martin Heidegger's existentialism. Bultmann insists that every interpreter is either consciously or unconsciously dependent upon certain philosophical assumptions and that since they are inescapable and none of them perfect in every respect, the exegete should select that philosophy which is most adequate conceptually for understanding human existence. Existential philosophy demonstrates its superiority at this point not by advocating a particular way in which man must exist, but by merely showing what it means to be.[14] Bultmann is persuaded that Heidegger's existential analysis can give new and vital meaning to some of the timeworn Christian concepts such as "faith," "spirit," "death," "sin," and "freedom."

The purpose for introducing Tillich and Bultmann to the reader has been to illustrate the manner in which two outstanding theologians of this century have utilized existentialist thought as an apologetic method in presenting the Christian message. This has not been an endeavor to summarize their theologies but merely to introduce two quite different methods-- the one correlating the philosophical questions with the Christian message, the other explicitly accepting the necessity of a particular philosophical pre-supposition in order to carry out an appropriate exe-getical task.[15] Bultmann has relied almost exclusive-ly upon Heidegger's analysis of the human condition in his interpretation of why and how the Christian message is important for contemporary man, whereas Tillich has been influenced in his approach by a number of existential thinkers, including Heidegger, and has relied much more upon his own resources and genius. A third theologian, John Macquarrie, will be the primary focus throughout the remainder of this chapter as illustrative of what is more likely to be a wide-spread utilization of existential theology.

However, before looking at the approach which Macquarrie takes to contemporary theologizing, a very brief sketch of the existentialist philosopher who has figured so important for both Bultmann and Macquarrie should be considered.[16]

HEIDEGGER

Martin Heidegger was born in Messkirch, the German province of Baden, in 1889.[17] His early experience in the life of a German agricultural community probably helped to account for a kind of earthiness of interest in poetry and religion which led him to study for the priesthood for a short time in a Jesuit seminary. However, before long he decided that his major in-terest lay not in the field of theology, but philoso-phy, and his education continued at the Gymnasium in Freiburg, and at the University of Freiburg where his doctoral dissertation dealt with the medieval philosopher Duns Scotus. He became a private lecturer at Freiburg in 1915. From 1923-28 he was Professor of Philosophy at the University of Marburg during which time the two great Protestant theologians, Paul Tillich and Rudolf Bultmann, were colleagues. In 1928 he was appointed Professor at Freiburg succeeding the renowned phenomenologist Edmund Husserl (1859-1938) from whom he had learned so much.

In 1933, after the National Socialist Party came into power, Heidegger was appointed Rector of the University of Freiburg but soon became disillusioned with the Nazi party and resigned his post in 1934. He remained Professor of Philosophy at the university until 1945, when he was forced to retire after Germany was taken over by the Allies. After that, he spent most of his life high up in the Black Forest mountains, not far from Freiburg, writing. He died in May, 1976. His major work <u>Being and Time</u> (1927),[18] is considered the most impressive analysis of human existence to have come out of the whole existentialist movement.

His Primary Concern

Heidegger's primary concern is with the meaning of "Being." Such a concern, philosophically speaking, is called "ontology." The classical philosopher endeavored to construct the nature of ontology by an analysis of the cosmos. Heidegger begins his construct of an ontology by an analysis of man, a particular being, or a peculiar instance of being.

The question of Being creates a good deal of confusion in the minds of many because it seems to imply that since we have the noun "Being" there must be some "thing" out there in the world that corresponds to it. Heidegger, however, insists that we cannot consider Being as an entity, or some thing that is. He insists that Being is not some category of substance (thinghood). He endeavors to clear away this notion of "thinghood" by mentioning three prejudices which tend to detract from an intelligent interest in the question about the meaning of Being.[19] It, first of all, does not refer to a property or class-concept such as "redness." It lies beyond all such class distinctions. Secondly, it is assumed that Being cannot be defined. This would be the case if

109

definitions had to identify the class, or genus, and specify the difference of that which is being defined. It certainly could not be defined if it were regarded as the most universal property or thing. But Heidegger asserts that the difficulty with defining Being merely indicates that Being cannot be comprehended as another thing which might be defined in the traditional manner. Rather, Being compels man to look for some way in which he can discuss its meaning. Thirdly, there is the prejudice which contends that Being is self-evident. While it is true that man does have some understanding of the term, it remains very vague and elusive. It is the philosopher's responsibility, according to Heidegger, to investigate dimly understood notions of Being and make them clear.

If man wishes to understand anything about the nature of Being, he must select something to examine which will lead to a greater understanding of its nature. The problem, however, is the broad expanse of entities or things, particular beings. What particular beings, or things--atoms, flowers, trees, or stars-- should he examine as the best manifestation of Being? Anything is a being of which it can be said that it is. Therefore, is there any one being whose qualities might be sufficiently outstanding as to make clear something more about the nature of Being in general? Heidegger asserts that there is and that such a being is found in the questioner himself--man. Man is uniquely qualified as a starting point for this investigation of Being because he not only is, but he has some understanding, of what it means "to be." However, because of man's measure of freedom and responsibility, the question of "Who am I?" is inescapable, and this question, if followed through with, leads inevitably to the prior question of Being in general. Man, in effect, is the ontological being.

"Being-there"

When Heidegger talks about man he uses the German word <u>Dasein</u> to call attention to man's ontological nature.[20] Literally, <u>Dasein</u> means "Being-there." This expression when applied to man calls attention to the finite, limited nature of man as the one who always finds himself in a specific situation. It, also, emphasizes that a man's thereness is his center of reference because he is "there." While <u>Dasein</u>

generally refers to "existence," Heidegger restricts its use to man's existence, and he restricts the use of "existence" to the kind of Being that belongs to "Being-there." Man is distinguished from all other beings because he not only is, but he has some perception of and responsibility for who he is. For Heidegger it is man alone who "exists." To "exist" means to "stand out" ("ex-sists") from the general structure of beings as that specific being who must decide about Being. "Dasein is an entity for which, in its Being, that Being is an issue."[21] Man's being is disclosed to him through his very mode of being.

However Heidegger asserts that it is only through the philosophical analysis of existence, by making clear the basic structures of being, that man can gain insight into his own being and the nature of Being in general. The method of his "existential analytic" is phenomenological.[22] Essentially, the phenomenological method is a careful, critical analysis of that which "shows itself in itself." It is a stripping away of everything that conceals so that things can be seen for what they are without distortion. It is not a method of "proof," but simply descriptive and, hopefully, revealing to all who look seriously.

Man as _Dasein_ is always in the world. _Dasein_ is always considered first of all as a concrete being and not as a mere thinking subject. "Being-in-the-world" constitutes the nature of _Dasein_.[23]

Heidegger's analysis of _Dasein_ reveals that there is a kind of threefold structure to existence which is exhibited in a general way in human existence as concern or "care."[24] First of all, the phenomena of _Dasein_ reveals itself in terms of potentiality or "possibility." Man's Being-in-the-world is such that it calls attention to his existence (his standing-out), especially in his awareness and responsibility he exhibits a unique degree of freedom. To exist authentically man must recognize the boundary of his existence which is "death." In so doing man, according to Heidegger, recognizes existence as his own existence.[25] To discover the meaning of his own being and to order his potentialities accordingly is, says Heidegger, the "authentic" understanding of Being. Secondly, the phenomena of _Dasein_ reveals itself as

"facticity." Man finds himself as thrown into existence and left to orient himself as best he can to
the world around him. He is not pure possibility,
but he is burdened with many givens which condition
and restrict his choices and potentialities. Heidegger insists that the direction in which man must
develop his possibilities is not given to him in
theoretical reason but rather in the various moods
of his Being, of which the basic one is anxiety.
Thirdly, Dasein reveals the phenomena of "fallenness." Man tends to fall away from what is most
distinctive in his existence. Man may deteriorate
into an absorption in the world of external objects.
His existence may be reduced to an instrumental level
in which all his needs and interests are subordinated
to things, or dominated by the depersonalized collective masses. His intellect may be sacrificed by
his attraction to the new simply for the sake of its
novelty. Such an existence Heidegger characterizes
as "unathentic." It is the suppression of "authentic"
selfhood by its everyday Being-in-the-world.

Temporality - the Model

Since "thinghood," or substance, is not an acceptable model for the understanding of Dasein, according to Heidegger, what model does he propose
that will make clear the structure of existence and
selfhood? Heidegger suggests that "temporality" is
the answer to this question.[26] Temporality happens
to correspond to the threefold structure of "care"
as the present (which correlates with fallenness),
the past (which correlates with facticity as that
which is given), and the future (which correlates
with possibility). Temporality, also, brings into
focus the distinction between "Being-there" (Dasein)
and animals or other beings or things. For example,
the relation of a substance such as a rock to time
is an external relation. It endures through time.
It is in time and, while it changes with time, its
future is "not yet" and its past is "no longer."
The existent, on the other hand, takes time and has
time and is not merely in time. He is not simply con-
fined to the "now" as is the thing. It is his inwardness that makes it possible for him to transcend time--
to contemplate his future, as well as his past.

Death - The Boundary

At the outset of this discussion it was stated
that the meaning of Being was all-important for
Heidegger. Now it must be asked, "What is its meaning?" As indicated above, anxiety is the basic mood
of man's being. Anxiety makes man aware of his
finitude, of which the most obvious sign is his death,
as well as his responsibility for his own existence.
Death is the boundary that marks off _Dasein_, as Being-
in-the-world, from the negation, or nothing, into
which it disappears when it ceases to be there. It
is at this point that Heidegger's ontological and
existential philosophies become linked together. It
is the concrete encounter of the "nothing" which man
has in his own being that gives rise to the notion
that pure undifferentiated Being is sheer nothingness. So, Being (as an all-inclusive notion) cannot
itself be considered as a being, or as something which
is. Rather, Being for Heidegger plays the same positive role for his ontology as death plays in his existential analysis. "It is," to quote Macquarrie,
"the non-entity which nevertheless has more being
than any entity, for it is the Being that comes before
every entity and in virtue of which any entity is."[27]

According to John Macquarrie,[28] Heidegger's
notion of the meaning of Being has something of a
divine, or holy character to it. It is "wholly other."
It is transcendent, beyond comprehension, and strikes
awe in the mind of man as he is driven to ask the
basic ontological question: "Why is there something,
rather than nothing?" It is approachable only by
"primordial" or "essential" thinking (which reflects
on Being, rather than beings, and is passive and receptive in character), rather than "calculative"
thinking (which objectifies, predicts, and controls
empirical events). As in negative theology "God"
is beyond the grasp of the human mind, but still the
ground of all intelligible understanding of existence,
so the same is true for Heidegger's notion of Being.
And, despite its negative character, Heidegger's
account of Being introduces affirmative concepts such
as "emerging" and "presence."

With this brief sketch of Heidegger's notion about
Being and _Dasein_ perhaps enough has been said to indicate the philosophical possibilities of his thought

for an apologetic theology. The contemporary theologian who has pursued such possibilities the farthest
is a former Professor of Systematic Theology at Union
Theological Seminary in New York City, John Macquarrie.

MACQUARRIE

John Macquarrie certainly went a long way towards establishing himself as an existentialist
scholar when he, in cooperation with Edward Robinson,
translated Martin Heidegger's magnum opus, Sein und
Zeit (Being and Time) into English. A very difficult
book, even for the German reader, many people considered the work "untranslatable." Macquarrie, born
in Renfrew, Scotland, in 1919, is the author of numerous books, scholarly articles, and a prominent
lecturer both in this country and abroad. His formal
education took place in Scotland, where he received
the M.A., B.D., and Ph.D. degrees at the University
of Glasgow. He is an ordained minister of both the
Church of Scotland and the Episcopal Church, and began
his ministerial career in St. Ninian's Church, Brechin,
Scotland, where he served from 1948 to 1953. From
1953 to 1962 he was a Lecturer in Systematic Theology at the University of Glasgow. In 1962 he became
Professor of Systematic Theology at Union Theological
Seminary where he taught until 1970. Since 1972 he has
been Lady Margaret Professor of Divinity at Oxford
University, Oxford, England. He is the recipient of
four honorary degrees, two of them from his alma mater
the University of Glasgow.

Macquarrie's most systematic and mature presentation of existential theology is set forth in his book
Principles of Christian Theology (1966). A lighter
treatment of some of his best thought on theology is
found in his book The Faith of The People of God:
A Lay Theology (1972).

His Theological Method

In contrast to John Cobb, who insists that process philosophy is the only suitable basis for a
Christian apologetic theology, Macquarrie is much
more aware of the ambiguous nature of all philosophical premises. Indeed, he declares that the "reality" of God or the "truth" of faith cannot be established by empirical arguments.[29] Futhermore,
he believes that there are probably several valid

114

approaches to both philosophy and theology.[30] In light of these attitudes it seems logical to ask: "Why, then, does Macquarrie use an apologetic approach to theology?" And, why, indeed, does he specifically select what is essentially a Heideggerian "ontological-existential" philosophy for his major theological position? With regards to this last question it is interesting to note that Macquarrie believes that Heidegger's philosophy is clearly a religious one, and one which endeavors to work out a contemporary faith position outside traditional Christian beliefs.[31] Is this the reason why Macquarrie appropriates the Heideggarian philosophy, or is there another reason?

The immediate task is to answer the preceeding questions. The remainder of this chapter will be used to indicate the major ways in which Macquarrie believes existential philosophy is appropriate as a means of making the Christian message clear in these times.

Man must always endeavor to demonstrate the logic of his faith whether that faith be of a religious nature or of a secular nature. According to Macquarrie, a natural theology, or apologetic theology, tries to establish foundations for theological discourse. A "reasonable faith" does not allow too little or too much to reason, but seeks to expose itself to an ongoing scrutiny and testing which will provide corrective measures. So even though reason cannot establish a religious faith, it can play a supportive role in the continued vitality and viability of a faith. Macquarrie asserts that this is precisely the function of contemporary apologetics. The apologetic theologian tries to bring the observable "facts" of the world in which he lives into harmony with the convictions of the faith.[32]

Whereas the old style natural theology tried to go too far with reason, by establishing deductive "proofs" of God, immortality, or whatever else seemed necessary, the new style natural theology (which Macquarrie prefers to call "philosophical theology")[33] takes a descriptive and existential approach to the world of being. Although philosophical theology, like the old natural theology, does not escape a final ambiguity (since its conclusions are, also,

lacking in ultimate certainty), yet it presses to
examine the conditions that lie behind the traditional
arguments. It also employs a different method, the
phenomenological, which lets man see "that which shows
itself (the phenomenon) by removing, as far as possible, concealments, distortions, and whatever else
might prevent him from seeing the phenomenon as it
actually gives itself."[34] Thus, for Macquarrie,
philosophical theology provides the link between
man's everyday thinking and experience and those
matters about which the theologian is concerned.
And, even though the picture presented to man by
his world about the final nature of reality is obscure, equivocal, or uncertain, it may serve a confirmatory purpose for the seeker or faithful.

However, the second question, which was set
forth above, asked why Macquarrie appropriates what
is basically Heidegger's brand of existentialism?
The short answer to the question is that he believes
that the "ontological-existential" philosophy is particularly appropriate at this time in history for two
reasons: First of all, it begins with man, who is
radically temporal, and not with some abstract theory.
Secondly, it provides the theologian with both a contemporary language and principles for interpretation.
Man, therefore, must try to set aside his preconceptions and favorite interpretations and let the
phenomena of human existence show themselves as they
are; he must strive to view the phenomena fairly and
objectively and suspend evaluation and interpretation of the phenomena until they have given themselves, then he may turn to the exacting task of interpretation. Even so the task of description is
extremely difficult and liable to error because of
the equivocal, ambiguous character of human existence.
Nevertheless, Macquarrie contends that man's existence is the appropriate starting point for an apologetic theology.[35]

Man as Standing-Out

Following the Heideggerian analysis Macquarrie
asserts that the primary meaning of man's "existence"
is the notion of "standing-out."[36] Man is uniquely
conscious of his being among other beings. He is
aware of his own awareness in a way that makes it a
problem for himself--he must accept responsibility

for his own possibilities, within limits. There is a persistent kind of openness about man's being. While there are specific "givens" in his nature which make him very much aware of his kinship with other animals, he is so transparent to himself that he is keenly aware of giving direction to his own evolution. It is this consciousness of responsibility that presents itself either as a burden or a possibility for man which creates the polarities or tensions of his existence. But these tensions or polarities are not simply between man and other beings, they are within existence itself.

Macquarrie presents four sets of polarities which he believes the phenomena of existence show.[37] Man stands out, first of all, as "possibility and facticity." Man is both free and bound. Man's nature or "selfhood" is not something that is already made, so to speak, but is always in the process of becoming. As an existent, man stands before great possibilities for deciding, commiting, acting, and responding to life. However, his potentialities for freedom are never without limits. He is always restricted to some degree by his heredity, environment, and society. His race, sex, intelligence, time and place in history, geographical location, temperament, and many other "givens" offset his freedom. So existence is always characterized by the tensions between freedom and finiteness.

Closely related to this first polarity is that between "rationality and irrationality." Unless man can be said to have the qualities of discrimination, judgment, understanding, and interpreting, there is no point in saying anything further about him, since such qualities are presupposed in any discussion. However, man's mind seems to be characterized by frequent self-deception, error, and operations which often defy explanation. Man's dream of creating a neat, orderly, logical, rational kind of world is always frustrated by expanding conditions of disorder, and threatening chaos. Man often fails to understand his own motives for action. He is both rational and irrational.

A third set of polarities which the phenomena of existence makes clear to man is that between "community and individuality." Community, as well as in-

dividuality, is intrinsic to existence. This fact is
well illustrated by man's biological life, especially
in the realm of reproduction, his economic life, and
his dependence upon language. These all drive man
toward community as a goal for survival, as well as
for some degree of humanization. At the same time a
man's existence is his own existence and his ego makes
him acutely aware of his own separate, private world
of experiences. Again, this polarity sets up tremendous tensions within and between the lives of men.

A final polarity which the phenomena of existence
shows to man is the opposition between "responsibility
and impotence." As already indicated, while there are
numerous beings which are--such as dogs, trees, and
rocks--only man is shown to exist (to "stand out")
according to the existential analysis. Responsibility
belongs to this existent who stands out. Macquarrie
contends that the mode of opening up of being which is
most closely connected with responsibility is "conscience."[38] It is conscience which makes man aware
of whether or not he is fulfilling his own potentialities as being, or measuring up to his possibilities.
Merely knowing what he should do does not imply that
man will do it. So the opposition against which responsibility must move is that of impotence, which
tends to destroy moral life and negate all aspirations. While the elements of facticity, irrationality, and individuality may all be involved here, Macquarrie asserts that impotence has a certain distinctiveness of its own which must be faced.

The Real Picture of Man

The existential analysis, thus far, shows human
existence to have an ambiguous, equivocal character.
It shows what is possible for human existence rather
than what it actually is. What is the actual picture
of existence when it is inspected?

Whether the focus is upon the community or the
individual, the picture is one of massive disorder.
More precisely it can be called an "imbalance,"
because it does not maintain an even tension in the
polar opposites as described.[39] This imbalance
occurs in two major directions, although an infinite
variety of combinations of distortions can take place.

On the one hand are those imbalances, or disorders, which take place when the individual or
society tends to deny or acknowledge the facticity
and limitations of human existence. For the most
part this disorder is more characteristic of individuals than it is of the masses. The individual becomes intoxicated by his own possibilities and rationality and seeks a godlike status--bewitched by his
own sense of power. (In the Christian tradition,
at least since the time of Augustine in the fourth
century, this phenomenon has been called "pride.")
On the other hand, there are those imbalances in
human existence which result when man moves in the
direction of the subhuman mode of being. The individual, or the society, seeks to escape higher possibilities through sensualism, insensitivity, despair,
or collective irresponsibility. While the existential
analysis would deny John Calvin's extreme claim that
man is totally "corrupt," or disordered, it does affirm or show a very deep disorder in the human condition which is universal in scope.

However, there are other models which can be used
to describe some of the subtleties of the human disorder other than that of "imbalance." A model which
is used by Martin Heidegger (see above), even though
its origin is from mythology and religion, is that
of "falling." It suggests falling away from authentic,
or genuine human actualization. Another model used by
Heidegger, and many other writers, is that of "alienation." It suggests a turning away from one or another
of the poles of human existence which leads to a distortion within existence itself. The basic alienation
is from the self (man fails to regard seriously his
full range of possibilities and limitations), which
in turn leads to alienation from others (his individual concerns override collective concerns), and which
in turn may lead to a sense of alienation from all
being. This sense of being cut off from self, others,
and the whole scheme of existence--a sense of having
no place in the world--is often called "lostness."[40]

As was indicated earlier, one part of the value
found in the ontological-existential philosophy is
its contemporary description of situations in which
theological terms and conditions take on renewed
meaning. Up to this point the discussion and description of the human situation has been carried on

in what Macquarrie would call "secular" language. Now it has become apparent that the condition which has been described as "falling," "alienation," and "lost-ness" is in religious or theological language known as "sin." According to Macquarrie, it is the idea of "lostness," of alienation from self, others, and, at a still deeper level, from God, which most sharply characterizes the notion of "sin." But since up to this point the descriptive method of theology has not studied the idea of "Being and God," Macquarrie breaks off the discussion of sin except for asking whether the description seems to fit the condition. (The second major division of Macquarrie's systematic approach to theology takes up Symbolic Theology which deals with the interpretation of the traditional sym-bols and images in which the "revealed truths of faith" are discussed.[41] This section of his work corresponds to what is traditionally called dogmatic theology and treats the concepts of the Trinity, God, Christ, man, etc.)

The phenomenological picture of human existence up to this point indicates a radical imbalance in man's being. There are those philosophers who, like Jean-Paul Sartre, bluntly contend that man's existence is self-contradictory. In Sartre's well known words "man is a useless passion."[42] Therefore, it is sense-less or absurd to try to find significance in man's aspirations and potentialities. His existence will terminate in death which is the final triumph of the negative over whatever feeble positive forces might show themselves in man's life. However, Heidegger, as well as other existentialists, insist that the disorders of human existence can be understood as a problem of "temporality"--with its three dimensions of past, present, and future--and that indications for a solution to the disorder of human existence is pos-sible. How, then, might existence fulfill itself under the Heideggarian scheme?

Human Fulfillment

To "exist" means to "stand out" from the general structure of beings as that specific being who must decide about Being. What is given man at the outset of his being is not a ready-made nature but a pos-sibility for becoming an "authentic" self. What really constitutes existence (personal being, <u>Dasein</u>)

is its connection with "temporality" (Being-in-the World). Temporality has three dimensions to it which correlate with the basic structers of existence--the present (fallenness), the past (facticity), and the future (possibility). When man cuts himself off from one or more of the temporal dimensions of existence, his existence declines into a disruption or imbalance of his being approximating that of things or animals. On the other hand, when man fulfills his potentialities as an existent being he holds the three dimensions of temporality together in a unity. He maintains their tension and balance. Such an existence is what Heidegger has called "authentic" existence and is not something given at birth, or ready made for man. It is an orderly actualization of potentialities with no alienated areas. In existence, therefore, this unity is never fully achieved but is always a matter of degree.

Is it possible to characterize the kind of unity found in authentic selfhood more completely? Two attitudes seem to be necessary to bring about an actual unity in the existent being. The one is "commitment" and the other is "acceptance."[43] The existent finds himself thrown into being and is forced to make sense of it, or to declare with Sartre that it is all absurd. A committed existence looks to the possibilities of the future being. It formulates some comprehensive possibility for existence and then subordinates all other possibilities to it. In its commitment to the central goal for its being the self actualizes its highest degree of unity and avoids the fragmentation which results from following impulsive decisions and chance commitments. However, of equal importance for human existence in the development of its possibilities is its acceptance of the facticity of its entire situation. Man must accept the totality of his existence, what has been, and what presently is, if he is to look realistically to his future possibilities. A strong commitment which denied the factical situation of man would be extremely disruptive and counterproductive.

In contrast to Sartre,[44] Heidegger insists that death, as a part of the factical situation of man, must be integrated into the possibilities of existence. Death more than anything else in existence makes man aware of his finitude, and it is precisely

in the light of this final limitation upon existence
that every possibility must be considered. Because
death is the end of existence, it brings into sharp
focus a seriousness and a responsibility for temporal
existence which it would not have otherwise. In this
sense it becomes creative of an ordered, responsible
selfhood. At the same time, death becomes a norm
for judging or evaluating superficial and trivial
concerns and ambitions as opposed to the central
issues of existence. In the light of those polarities
of human existence which have been considered it becomes clear that when a man gives himself completely
to sensuality, for example, he not only distorts existence, but the fact of death makes vivid the fleeting
and frivolas character of his achievements when the
full range of his potentialities and limitations are
taken into account.

The Broader Context - Faith

It is precisely this awareness that death shows
up the futility of existence which compels Sartre to
assert that it is the final absurdity of life. The
contrasting views of the significance of death simply
points out its ambiguous character. Is death to be
understood in a negative or a positive sense? The
discussion of death suggests that man may have to
look beyond his own being, to a wider context, in
order to find a way to authentic existence. In short,
it raises the religious concern of man, the ultimate
concern, as to the meaning of existence. It raises
the issue of faith. Human existence can make sense
only if there is some broader context in which to
consider it--only if there is a supportive Being beyond finite being. This brings man back to the importance of commitment and acceptance. Faith is not
merely believing, but it involves most of all an acceptance of the unprovable and a commitment to a
"wider being"--a Being beyond finite being. Faith
demands an existential attitude. It demands taking
human existence very seriously despite the risks involved!

According to Macquarrie, the ontological-existential analysis, up to this point, demonstrates that
man's quest for authentic selfhood, or wholeness, and
a meaningful existence is not a luxury but inherent
in being.[45] Man, the finite being, is thrown into

existence but is able to see it only from within.
Therefore, he cannot know with certainty what to make
of the enigma of human existence--its polarities, disorders, self-contradictions--but he cannot negate the
necessity, as an existent, of coming to some decision
about it. To exist means that man has already choosen
some action, some goals, some standards of value,
some way of understanding himself. The limiting
extremes as to how man may understand himself appear
to be either the religious faith or a Sartrean acceptance of life's absurdity. Which will it be? Is
it just a toss-up as to which attitude a man accepts--
theism or acute atheism?

The only procedure for settling the question,
asserts Macquarrie, is to look at the picture described by the philosopher as carefully as possible
and then see if it really seems to fit human existence.
As an existential theologian Macquarrie would focus
attention, especially, upon such structures of human
existence as its disorders, its awareness of "lost-
ness," its need for cooperation with being, and the
quest for meaning.

Macquarrie contends that the biblical picture
of man and that picture given by the ontological-
existential analysis have sufficient affinity to
assure a justifiable comparison. First of all, the
biblical picture of man certainly recognizes man's
distinctiveness. Man is recognized as created in the
"image of God" (the doctrine of the imago Dei).[46] Man,
indeed, does "stand out" from other beings. Macquarrie declares that this concept of the imago Dei
is actually better communicated in the contemporary
language of "existence" than in the traditional manner. To "exist" is to have an "openness" to love, to
responsibility, to creativity. Man is that being,
or creature, whose existence allows him to move outward to other beings. His imago Dei is not something
fixed, or static, but must be thought of more in terms
of potentiality, and possibilities, and freedom.

At the same time, the Biblical picture of man
portrays the polarities of human existence. He is
free and bound, spirit and flesh, responsible and
guilty, rational and irrational. He is recognized
as an individual but is always linked with community.

He is certainly a creature with continuity to other creatures but is, likewise, the shaper of nature and the controller of it.

The biblical picture of man's propensity for disorder, of "imbalance," is certainly as sharp as is that of the existentialist. Despite man's possibilities for greatness as "sons of God," with his capacity for love, freedom, and responsibility, he has an ever present impotence. Man inevitably fixes upon one or the other poles of his existence and becomes a being for self rather than others, or a being of indulgence in things, in the past (facticity), rather than holding the polarities in unity with temporality. The classical biblical term for this condition is "sin."[47] Man is a sinner. Man is alienated from his own being, the being of others, and from the ground of Being (God). And, while the condition is individual, it is universal in scope.

Ontologically expressed, in his quest for Being, which arises out of the very constitution of existence, man turns his attention to particulars (creatures, beings) rather than to the abstract universal (Being or God).[48] While Heidegger calls it a "forgetting of Being," theologically speaking it is "idolotry." It is man's inclination to find the strength of his existence or the meaning of his existence in self, or in finite entities alone. It is a kind of distorted faith, because it involves a commitment. Man becomes committed to an idolizing of himself or his creations. He aspires to play God-- to supplant Being. This attitude leads to various expressions of pride which is very destructive of human community and interpersonal relations in general.

Existence is from the beginning individual, but it is also communal. The biblical Adam was incomplete until the creation of Eve. The ontological-existential philosophy and the biblical view both recognize the basic inseparableness of the individual and the community. This inseparableness is recognized as applicable both in the realm of disorder (sin) and in the realm of responsibility. Man, as well as mankind, is fallen or "lost," and both share the guilt for a massive disorder and perversion of human existence. Consequently, there is a kind of impotence ("original sin") within the human condition which man is not able to rectify and which sends him in search of "grace."[49] The very fact that man is aroused for this quest is, according to Macquarrie, a strong witness against the Calvinistic doctrine that man is completely and totally depraved.

The problem of the quest for grace (which will be dealt with later) is taken care of in the Christian tradition in the doctrines of Revelation and Reconciliation. While the doctrine of Revelation will be discussed later in this chapter, the Christian answer to the problem of human fulfillment must be briefly mentioned.

The activity whereby the alienations, the disorders, the imbalances of human existence are dealt with in the Christian message is in the doctrine of "reconciliation." Reconciliation is the making whole, or the healing of the total man. It is the bringing of man into a wholesome relationship with God, himself, and others. It is God's saving activity in the world which He, and He alone, initiates by his self-disclosure, or revelation. For the Christian faith the decisive model, or "symbol" of Being, wherein the manifestation of God's presence and activity are disclosed to man is the Christ.[50] Man needs a concrete expression of God's intensions for him in order to bring him into an attitude of faith. In the Christ, man is able to receive a renewed vision of existence and self-understanding which leads him into an experience of self-fulfillment and harmony with God. God's creative work in man is expressed in the Christ as self-giving, as the absolute "letting-be," self-emptying, or love.[51] And it is in the new community founded on Christ that the creative reconciling work of Christ's love continues.[52]

The Quest for Being - "grace"

However, the discussion of man's possibilities for reconciliation presupposes an act of faith which in turn is related to the quest for Being or "grace." Man, that unique being who "stands-out" from other things, does not find satisfaction in beings, but is driven on to the quest of Being. But the quest does not lead him to a final certainty, and he is doomed either to the frustration of despair, or he

asserts that his destiny must find its fulfillment
in some wider Being beyond the finite. This vague
awareness that man's selfhood cannot be fulfilled
within the structures of temporality has been characteristic of man throughout his history. It has often
been described as a kind of natural religious inclination within man and expressed in various ways, such
as the restlessness of the heart until it finds its
rest in God (Augustine), or the ultimate concern which
every man has (Tillich). However, the religious man,
or the man of faith, tends to feel that the object
of his quest is not something for which he must search
so much as it is something which is, likewise, seeking him or meeting him. It is often expressed as an
experience of being "grasped" by faith.

As indicated earlier, the search for a meaningful, existence, the quest for Being, arises out of
man's very constitution as being. The tensions between
the polarities and the ease with which man falls into
disorders, as he follows his inclinations to move
out to one extreme or another in his endeavor to
realize fulfillment, throws man into a state of anxiety.[53] The existentialists contend that there is a
heightening of this anxiety as man becomes more aware
of the disorder and guilt of his existence. The source
of this basic uneasiness or malaise is man's awareness of his transience and finitude. It is his consciousness of the "nothingness" into which his life
may lapse--the awareness of the precariousness of
existence, the emptiness of his being. The world
gets stripped of the meanings, the values, the sense
which man assigns to existence within it. And, despite the illusions and technology which man creates
to tranquilize himself against the oppressiveness of
this condition in his existence, it persists. Macquarrie contends that the mood is universal and even
though not generally prevailing it catches up with
everyone at some time.

Anxiety, because it tends to intensify man's
particular predicament as well as his total situation
in the world, sets the stage for his receptivity to
revelation. "It predisposes us," declares Macquarrie,
"to recognize the approach of holy being."[54] As
Heidegger asserts, it can function as that which
approaches "awe" for man.[55] It not only serves to
draw man's attention to the negativity of his being,

but may call his attention to the positive possibility
of the grace of being. It opens man's eyes to the
wonder of being--the "creature feeling" which man
recognizes in the presence of the holy (Rudolf Otto).[56]
In other words, anxiety arouses in man the essential
characteristics of faith--acceptance and commitment.
Faith is primarily this existential attitude.

The Quest for Being - "holy being"

But what is it that reveals itself to man when
he is caught up with this sense of the nothingness
of himself and his world? Briefly, it is the being
in virtue of which all other beings are. In terms of
the content of revelation it is what Macquarrie calls
"holy being," or "God."[57]

From the standpoint of philosophical theology
there are three comments which Macquarrie makes about
this description of revelation. First of all, any
revelatory experience must be concrete and particular,
but he does not restrict it to biblical revelation.
For revelation to occur, it must occur at a particular
time, at a particular place, with particular symbols,
and to a specific person(s). However, it does not
have to be the biblical experience of a Moses at the
burning bush, or the acceptance of Jesus, by Peter,
as the Christ. It might just as well be the acceptance of Muhammad by a disciple. Secondly, what
the person who sees the revelation sees is not some
Superbeing whom others cannot see, rather he sees an
added dimension of that which others ignore or refuse
to see. He simply sees in a new way, or different
way, that which is present to others who are looking.
Thirdly, Macquarrie makes a distinction between "primordial" revelations upon which faith communities are
founded (such as the recognition of the early disciples
that Jesus was the Messiah), and "repetitive" revelations which sustain the ongoing life of faith communities. The latter type of revelation is the most
common and it consists, essentially, of a re-living
of the insights and possibilities perceived by the
original or "primordial" community.[58]

Macquarrie contends that philosophical theology
must try to show where the experience of revelation
belongs within the entire field of knowing (or epis-

127

temology). This he does by following what is, basically, Heidegger's approach concerning different types of thinking (which was indicated earlier in this chapter). The first level of thinking Heidegger calls "calculative"--a type of subject-objective approach in which the object is manipulated, used, or controlled. It computes, organizes and plans.[59] The second level Macquarrie calls "existential" thinking-- a type of subject-subject approach, which involves "participation," or a "thinking into" the other person's experience. This is the proper kind of thinking in relation to other persons. It corresponds to the "I-thou" thinking of Martin Buber which rests upon the mutuality and affirmation of one subject (person) by another subject. At the same time, this way of thinking may become theoretical where calculative interests are subordinated to the practical interests of existence, such as in the existential analytic procedure of Heidegger.

A unique instance of existential thinking is to be found in "repetitive" revelation. Even though Macquarrie does not believe that this is the best mode of thinking in order to understand the primal experience of revelation, he acknowledges that for the great majority of people faith arises through this kind of encounter--through the testimony of the community of the faithful.[60] His rejection of this personal language as the way for knowing or understanding revelation is based upon the fact that man's encounter with "Being" (or "God") is not the same as man's encounter with man. The encounter with "God" is not the meeting of another being, nor is it a reciprocal experience.[61]

It is in a third type of knowing and understanding which Macquarrie considers most helpful in thinking about the revelatory experience. This is the kind of thinking which Heidegger calls "primordial" or "essential" thinking. It is the kind of thinking which opens up man to the mystery of being. In contrast to calculative thinking "primordial" thinking is reflective, it "waits" and "listens," it is receptive and responsive.[62] This kind of philosophical thinking provides Macquarrie with the basic model for understanding what is meant by the concept of "revelation." It indicates, also, where to locate the cognitive experience of revelation. For the philosopher, and the religious man as well, the meeting of Being seems to have a "gift-like" quality to it. The initiative comes from that which is beyond man and impresses itself upon him as "grace" or a gift of wonderment. However, it can never be an entirely passive experience because all knowing involves a degree of participation or appropriation. Macquarrie insists, always, that man must have a capacity for revelation or it could never take place.

At this point it should be clear that for Macquarrie faith is not basically assent to dogmatic assertions, but a commitment and acceptance characterized by involvement. It should be clear, also, that revelation is primarily a self-giving of being to man. Macquarrie declares that the content of this revelation is "holy being." But this leaves the content of revelation so vague that there is reason to doubt whether anything has been revealed to man. Therefore, something more must be said about the nature of being if "holy being" is to have any meaning.

In the clearest and most affirmative terms, Macquarrie contends that there are three primary concepts that are revealed by the notion of being.[63]

First of all, since being is not the sum of beings, a class of beings, or a being, or a material thing, it must be regarded as strictly unique. Since it does not fall under any of the usual categories of comprehension, Macquarrie insists that it is a "prior condition" which transcends all categories.

Secondly, being is "letting-be." While being "is" not, in the literal sense of things, it enables, or empowers, or brings into being. "Letting-be" is prior to the instance of being. Therefore, man is justified in claiming that being is greater and takes priority to any particular being it empowers or "lets be."[64] For the same reason Macquarrie contends that the expression "being is" is justifiable when used in a proper symbolic manner. Since man cannot answer the question why is there "something" rather than "nothing," the ultimate "letting-be" is merely a part of the mystery of being. Still, this "letting-be" does not erase the basic ambiguity of the human experience. The man of faith, or religious man, experiences the letting-be as a gift, as grace which confirms his being; whereas someone else may experience letting-be as a burden or imposition which leads to despair.

Thirdly, Macquarrie contends that this mysterious letting-be makes man aware of something described as "presence" and "manifestation." Being, despite its prior and transcendent character, as that which is furthest from man is, also, experienced as that which is closest to man--presence. There is a sense of its participation in beings. While being is present in every particular being it may, nevertheless, remain hidden to man or it may become manifest to man in various ways. As indicated early in this chapter,[65] although being is not a being or a person, that being which most fully reveals the nature of being is man. Therefore, even though a molecule of gas and a well-integrated human are both beings that manifest or show being, it is the person who most fully manifests being. It is the human being who manifests the greatest range and possibilities of all known beings.

But what has this to do with Macquarrie's notion of "holy being?" Are the words "being" and "God" synonymous? No! Macquarrie declares that "being" is a neutral term whereas "God" is not. The term "God," while it designates being, also denotes certain existential valuations, commitments, and notions of worship; however, Macquarrie does use the term "God" as synonymous with "holy being."[66]

Macquarrie relies heavily upon the philosophy of Heidegger in coming to this analysis of being as the present and manifest power which "lets-be."[67] As indicated earlier Heidegger's own philosophy of being appears to replace "God" with being.[68] Macquarrie contends that Heidegger's objection to the use of the term "God" is on the grounds that it has become identified with a being, or some being in addition to the world. Macquarrie insists that on these grounds such an objection is justified and that contemporary theology is beginning to move toward Heidegger in this respect. His own theology is, of course, a deliberate effort to do this very thing. He wishes to demonstrate that a new level of intelligibility and relevance will be brought to bear upon many traditional Christian doctrines by the understanding of "God" as being rather than as "a being." Therefore, for philosophical theology the phrase "holy being," or the term "Being" (with the initial capital) can be used interchangeably with the term "God."[69]

Religious Language - a Problem

Before concluding this chapter on existential theology a few remarks must be made concerning the importance of the "ontological-existential" language for the interpretation of religious symbols in Macquarrie's thought. These remarks are of particular importance for understanding the traditional religious notion that "God exists." If God is not to be thought of as some exalted being, or a particular being, in what sense can it be said that He "exists?"

The justification of theological language is based precisely upon the context out of which it arises--the community of faith. The language of theology endeavors to clarify the existential or faith experience of man as he moves from the questioning of his own being to the search for meaning and to the revelatory experience in which he is grasped by a sense of grace by Being itself. Theological language is very complex in its meaning because it endeavors to express the existential attitude of the whole self over the entire range of existence. Despite the fact that this language is loaded with valuations and feelings, it is obligated to be the vehicle of understanding, insight, and clarification by which man comprehends the incomprehensible--Being (or God). Consequently, theological and religious language abounds in modes of discourse which have "stretched" the language far beyond its customary usage.

Macquarrie notes that the peculiarity of theological and religious language can be recognized when the theologian uses such terms as "paradoxical," "mythological," "symbolical," or "analogical" to explain his meanings.[70] Language, of course, is intended to help man share his insights from experience, or whatever, with other men. But this sharing can take place only if men have a common frame of reference. Contemporary man often does not understand the communications of the faith community because he does not share in the experiences, practices, stories, doctrines and history to which it alludes, or he does not share in the presuppositions of, for instance, a particular myth. Consequently, communication often depends upon interpretation and interpretation demands two languages. Each language must illuminate the other. Therefore, the theologian who wishes to communicate with contemporary man and to interpret his faith to him must discover a language that will be as widely understood as possible. It must be a language whose frame of reference is open to all.[71]

What is this frame of reference which all men share as human beings? The answer to this question has been indicated numerous times in this discussion of "ontological-existential" theology as the analogy of being (analogia entis). However, even though Macquarrie (following Bultmann) insists that mythology has virtually no meaning for contemporary man,[72] man cannot escape the problems of symbolism. In the broadest sense all language has a symbolic character; therefore a few distinctions must be made to indicate the use of this term by the theologian. First of all, it must be distinguished from a literal language. Secondly, it must refer, for the most part, to intrinsic symbolizations rather than conventional or traditional symbolizations. Of course, any particular symbol operates within a more or less restricted group of people. There is probably no symbol that is completely private or one that is completely universal. All symbols require some interpretation. Thirdly, man will probably never be able to leave symbols behind completely; therefore the theologian must use those symbols which embrace the widest possible understanding rather than the more restricted ones. It must always be remembered that interpretation is dependent upon two or more languages which illuminate one another.[73]

Symbolic theology proceeds with the interpretation of the likeness of being upon the assumption that beings, or a being, can never be completely separated from Being, nor assimilated to Being. While there could be no beings without that Being which lets them be, at the same time Being, apart from beings, would be indistinguishable from nothingness. "Hence Being and the beings, though neither can be assimilated to the other, cannot be separated from

each other."[74] However, the symbols involved in the
analogy of being must be looked at from two sides.

First of all, Macquarrie looks at the symbols
from the side of particular beings.[75] These symbols
are qualities, things, and persons which arouse the
existential attitude in man. They awaken a sense of
commitment or reverence in man. Again, looked at from
the side of beings, these symbols make apparent some
"similarity of relation." For instance, the analogy
of God (Being) as a father points to the relationship
of dependence which the child has with the father.
Such analogues do not, to be sure, disclose Being
"as it is in itself," but they do point to something
in the relationship which is very authentic in terms
of an existential-ontological analysis. The same
would be true of such symbols, or analogues, as "goodness" or "wisdom," if they are viewed in terms of a
similarity of relationship and not as properties or
characteristics of Being as such.

However, since Being is not a being, or a thing,
it does not have properties or beingness. Can any
sense be made, therefore, of the notion that God is
"good," "wise," or that God "is?" Macquarrie insists
that such symbols are valid if thought of in terms
of Being as the "prior enabling condition."[76] Being
as that necessary source or condition which makes
beings possible has more "beingfulness" than any
single being or property. Clearly the language here
cannot be used literally, but symbolically. Being
(or God) as that which "lets be" rather than "is,"--
as the prior condition for "isness"--can be more
appropriately thought of as "existing" than as "not
existing." Even though God does not "exist," in the
sense that man "exists," he is the prior condition
for "existence."

But do these analogues or symbols really bridge
the gulf between the divine Being and the beings of
which man ordinarily speaks? Not really, says Macquarrie, until man turns to the other side of the
analogy of Being.[77] How might Being disclose itself
symbolically to man?

Being, when understood as that which gives
itself through and with and in a being or beings, is
not some entity that exists in addition to the beings

known in everyday experience. Rather, Being is "manifest" in the beings that it lets be. Being participates in or makes itself present to beings. The symbol is not literally that which it symbolizes, otherwise it would not be a symbol, but it makes the other apparent. Every particular being is a clue to Being, not because it is like Being, but because it participates in and expresses Being. However, this raises the critical question of what being, or beings, best manifests or symbolize Being? There are certain classic symbols which are given in primordial revelation to the faith community--such as the cross, the fatherhood of God, the Messiah--which have their significance and meaning only within the context of a particular revelation of God. But aside from these, Macquarrie declares that some things are better suited to be symbols of Being than others.

According to Macquarrie, the real test of any symbol is the "adequacy" with which it illuminates that of which it is symbolic. As already indicated, it is man who participates in the widest range of being known--as material body, animal organism, and as person--who best symbolizes Being. In the Christian doctrine of incarnation, it is a person who symbolizes, or makes manifest, or illuminates, the nature of God (Being).[78] There is, therefore, a primacy that belongs to personal images and symbols, since they indicate the widest range of participation in Being. Nevertheless, Macquarrie notes that there is always a certain paradoxical element present in theological language.[79] Precisely because symbols are symbols they must be both affirmed and denied. Good symbols do illuninate what they symbolize but they still fall short.

Before concluding this chapter on existential theology there are a few observations and concerns which should be raised with respect to the adequacy of the approach.

John Macquarrie seems to have avoided a number of the dangers of the existential-ontological approach, to apologetic theology, by employing a rigorous, coordinated methodology to its content. His use of phenomenology and his stress upon the interpretative processes keep him from the excesses of irrationalism, amoralism, individualism, and the

radical subjectivity of some existentialists. He
uses his philosophical theology to clarify and illuminate the foundations of the faith experience,
rather than trying to "prove" God's existence by
deductive, rationalistic principles. He applies his
symbolic theology to the images, symbols, and dogmatic assertions of religious and Christian tradition
in an effort to bring about a contemporary interpretation and to expose the existential-ontological
roots of faith.

Macquarrie proceeds with the existential-ontological approach to theology fully aware of the
ambiguity of philosophical theology[80] and, yet, convinced that such an analysis must be carried out precisely because of the ambiguous, equivocal character
of all faith positions. He fully recognizes that
man's language about God is not literal, matter of
fact language--such as facts about the weather--and
demands the use of symbols, analogies, and even paradoxical statements. And yet, Macquarrie's overall
approach to systematic theology is so Anglo-Catholic
and traditional that he even treats the topic of angels
and seriously discusses the doctrine of purgatory.[81]
But, perhaps, even this may have a confirmatory affect
upon a man's faith.

The existential-ontological kind of theology
does appear to have several distinct advantages over
process theology. First of all, it begins with man;
and the question about man, that particular instance
of being, is still asked even though the question
about Being, or God, may not appear relevant. Dis-
cussing the possibilities and the limitations, and
hopes and despairs, the heights and the depths of
the human existent just may open up the dimension of
transcendence.[82] Secondly, it does offer a resource
for language by which many biblical and traditional
Christian and religious concepts can be expressed.
It, also, offers principles which assist man tre-
mendously in the articulation and the interpretation
of the faith experience in a scientific, technological
age. Thirdly, its radically realistic and pessimistic
view of man and his institutions serves a salutary
function in an age readily swayed by the scientific
myth of progress.

At the same time, existential-ontological analysis
may appear too pessimistic, or even morbid, about the

human situation. Existential theology may impress
many as too destructive of human hope and progress,
and out of step with this modern age of science.
It may appear to negate the hopes, aspirations, and
goals of those "third world" peoples, the unliberated
of the earth.

Finally, existential theology must seriously face
the question as to whether it is too narrowly human-
istic in its approach. Dasein (man) as the measure
of all things tends to minimize serious attention to
interests in the kinds of entities investigated by
the natural sciences. Perhaps the most serious affect
of such an attitude is a man-centered philosophy which
neglects or distorts man's relationship to the total
environment. Contemporary man needs a philosophy of
life, and a theology, which will treat seriously his
relationship and dependency upon nature.

FOOTNOTES

[1]Cf. John Macquarrie, _Existentialism_ (The Westminster Press, 1972), pp. 2-3.

[2]Cf. Macquarrie's survey of this matter _ibid._, Chapter Fourteen.

[3]For a psychiatric and psychological viewpoint of the existentialist see Rollo May, _et. al._, (eds.) _Existence: A New Dimension in Psychiatry and Psychology_ (Basic Books, Inc., 1958); for original works see Kierkegaard, _The Concept of Dread_, trans. by Walter Lowrie (Princeton University Press, 1944); Heidegger, _Being and Time_, trans. by J. Macquarrie and E. S. Robinson (Harper & Row, 1962); Sartre, _Being and Nothingness: An Essay on Phenomenological Ontology_ (Philosophical Library, 1956); and his _The Emotions: Outline of a Theory_, trans. by B. Frechtman (Philosophical Library, 1948).

[4]Cf. David E. Roberts, _Existentialism and Religious Belief_, edited by Roger Hazelton (Oxford University Press, 1957), pp. 6-8; and John Macquarrie, _op. cit._, pp. 12-16, for some of the general characteristics of existentialism.

[5]For an appreciative but critical interpretation of Kierkegaard of moderate length see Roberts, _op. cit._, Chapters II and III. For a more extensive study see Walter Lowrie, _Kierkegaard: A Life_ (Harper & Row, 1962), two vols.

[6]Cf. Samuel Enoch Stumpf, _Socrates to Sartre: A History of Philosophy_ (McGraw-Hill Book Co., 1966), Chapter 15.

[7]_Op. cit._, p. 42.

[8]For a brief fair treatment of the lives, thought, and contributions of both Paul Tillich and Rudolf Bultmann using a great deal of the primary sources see James C. Livingston, _Modern Christian Thought: From the Enlightenment to Vatican II_ (The Macmillan Company, 1971), Chapter Twelve. For a discussion of what Tillich means by "ultimate concern," and the "method of correlation," and the relationship of Theology and Philosophy see his _Systematic Theology_, Vol. I (The University of Chicago Press, 1951), pp. 8-28; 59-68; Vol. II, pp. 13-16.

[9]See Systematic Theology, Vol. II, p. 14.

[10]His little book _Jesus Christ and Mythology_ (Charles Scribner's Sons, 1958), is probably the best source for a full explanation of the method of "demythologizing."

11See Bultmann, _ibid._, p. 45.

12Cf. _ibid._, pp. 19-20; 35-36; also, see Bultmann, "New Testament and Mythology," in _Kerygma and Myth_, Vol. I, edited by Hans W. Bartsch (London: S.P.C.K., 1953 and 1962), pp. 1-2; 10-11.

13See _Jesus Christ and Mythology_, pp. 53-59.

14Cf. _ibid._, p. 55.

15An excellent comprehensive evaluation of Bultmann's demythologizing method can be found in John Macquarrie's book _The Scope of Demythologizing: Bultmann and his Critics_ (SCM Press, 1960).

16In his "Preface" to _Principles of Christian Theology_ (Charles Scribner's Sons, 1966), p. ix, John Macquarrie acknowledges his great indebtedness to Heidegger for the philosophical categories that make his contemporary "natural" theology possible, as well as the help he has received from the thought of Karl Rahner, a Roman Catholic theologian greatly influenced by Heidegger, and Rudolf Bultmann as his principal mentor in the understanding of the New Testament.

17For a brief biographical sketch of his life and thought see John Macquarrie, _Martin Heidegger_ (John Knox Press, 1968).

18Originally published in Germany under the title _Sein und Zeit_. It was translated by J. Macquarrie and E. S. Robinson and published in English in 1962 by Harper & Row, in this country, and the SCM Press, in England. For an extensive bibliography on Heidegger see J. Macquarrie, _Existentialism_, pp. 241-242.

19See _Being and Time_, pp. 22-24, or Macquarrie, _Martin Heidegger_, pp. 5-6.

20See the discussion by Macquarrie, _Martin Heidegger_, pp. 7, 12-14; also, Heidegger, _Being and Time_, p. 27.

21Heidegger, _Being and Time_, p. 236.

22Cf. Macquarrie, _Martin Heidegger_, p. 11; also, Heidegger, _Being and Time_, pp. 49-62, esp., 59-60.

23See Macquarrie, _ibid._, p. 14; also, Heidegger, _ibid._, p. 78-86.

24See Macquarrie, _ibid._, p. 27; also, Heidegger, _ibid._, esp., pp. 235-241.

25Heidegger's discussion of death and dying is a very interesting aspect of his philosophy. See Macquarrie, _ibid._, p. 30; also, Heidegger, _ibid._, pp. 279-311.

26See Macquarrie, _ibid._, p. 34; also, Heidegger, _ibid._, p. 374.

[27] Macquarrie, *ibid.*, p. 45.

[28] See his discussion, *ibid.*, pp. 45-50; 57-60.

[29] See Macquarrie, *God Talk* (Harper & Row, 1967), pp. 234, 244; also, *Principles of Christian Theology*, pp. 47-50.

[30] See Macquarrie, "Existentialism and Christian Thought," in *Philosophical Resources for Christian Thought*, ed. by Perry Lefevre (Abingdon Press, 1968), p. 128.

[31] See Macquarrie, *Martin Heidegger*, pp. 59-60. See also, *Principles of Christian Theology*, pp. 105-106.

[32] See *God Talk*, p. 234; also, cf. *Principles of Christian Theology*, Chapter II; and his *Twentieth-Century Religious Thought: The Frontiers of Philosophy and Theology, 1900-1960* (Harper & Row, 1963), p. 370; and "Existentialism and Christian Thought," in *Philosophical Resources for Christian Thought*, p. 139.

[33] See *Principles of Christian Theology*, pp. 48-52.

[34] *Ibid.*, p. 31.

[35] See *ibid.*, Chapter III.

[36] See *ibid.*, p. 54.

[37] See *ibid.*, pp. 56-58.

[38] See *ibid.*, p. 58.

[39] See *ibid.*, p. 60.

[40] See *ibid.*, pp. 61-62. The late Paul Tillich used the concept of "estrangement" to point out this basic characteristic of man's predicament in existence. See his *Systematic Theology*, Vol. II, pp. 44-75.

[41] See *Principles of Christian Theology*, pp. 161-330.

[42] *Being and Nothingness: A Essay on Phenomonological Ontology*, translated by Hazel E. Barnes (Philosophical Library, 1956), p. 615.

[43] See *Principles of Christian Theology*, p. 68.

[44] Cf. Sartre, *loc. cit.*, p. 627.

[45] Cf. *Principles of Christian Theology*, pp. 71 ff.

[46] See *ibid.*, pp. 212-213.

[47] See *ibid.*, pp. 237 ff.

[48] See *ibid.*, p. 238.

[49] Cf. *ibid.*, pp. 240-245.

[50] See *ibid.*, p. 249 f.

[51] See *ibid.*, p. 278.

[52] See *ibid.*, p. 292.

[53] See *ibid.*, pp. 77-78, 88-89.

[54] See *ibid.*, p. 78.

[55] See Macquarrie's reference *ibid.*, p. 89, footnote 11.

56Cf. The Idea of the Holy, translated by John
W. Harvey (Galaxy Book, 1958), pp. 5-30.
57See Principles of Christian Theology, Chapter V.
58Cf. ibid., pp. 80-81, 83.
59See ibid., pp. 82-86. Cf. Heidegger, Discourse
on Thinking, translated by John M. Anderson and E.
Hans Freund (Harper and Row, 1966), pp. 45-47.
60See ibid., p. 93.
61Cf. his arguments ibid., p. 84.
62See ibid., pp. 85-86. Cf. also Heidegger, Discourse on Thinking, pp. 54-56.
63See ibid., pp. 102-104.
64See ibid., p. 103.
65See supra., pp. 110-111.
66See Principles of Christian Theology, p. 105.
67See ibid.
68See supra., pp. 113-114.
69See Principles of Christian Theology, pp. 105-
107, 110.
70Cf. ibid., p. 117 f.
71See ibid., p. 118.
72Macquarrie acknowledges that mythology was the
pretheological language of religion and that Bultmann performed a great service to theology with his
demythologizing method. However, he faults Bultmann
because, despite his existential analysis of the myth
and his use of analogical language in talking about
"God's acts," and "God's address," he did not develop
the ontological significance of the myth. See ibid.,
pp. 120-122.
73Cf. ibid., pp. 122-125.
74Ibid., p. 126.
75See ibid., pp. 126-130.
76Ibid., p. 129, cf. his discussion on God as
existing, p. 108.
77Cf. ibid., pp. 130-132.
78See the discussion on the Christ, supra., p. 125.
79In God Talk, Macquarrie argues that while the
anologia entis language about God is by no means empty,
and does indeed relate to the reality of God, or divine
Being, yet it can be misleading. The theologian must
always keep in mind that the best of images or symbols
must be held dialectically, because God far exceeds
anything that the human mind can grasp. See p. 230.
Cf. Chapters 11 and 12.

[80]See _supra._, pp. 114-116.

[81]Cf. _Principles of Christian Theology_, pp. 215-218; 326-329.

[82]At least one current theologian believes this is possible. See Carl Skrade, _God and the Grotesque_ (The Westminster Press, 1974).

CHAPTER FIVE

PHENOMENOLOGICAL THEOLOGY

The history of man can almost be characterized
as the movements from one extreme to another. At
times he appears ascetic and rigidly self-controlled,
and at other times he appears sensualistic and self-
indulgent. He appears to move through eras of extremely rigid morality to times of loose morality,
from strictness to permissiveness, from conservative
to liberal, from spirituality to materialism. Certainly when the history of his ideas are looked at,
whether it be in the fields of philosophy, economics,
education, politics, literature, or religion, a dia-
letic appears quite obvious. While the process philosopher tends to invest too much certainty in the
notion of objective reality, the existentialist
thinker tends to assert too vigoriously the absolute-
ness of the inward or subjective nature of reality.
Since the times of Plato and Aristotle this debate
about the location and nature of reality has been
carried on by philosophers. The development of the
phenomenological movement might best be understood
as the endeavor to find a method of intellectual
analysis which would examine fairly the subjective
reality of that which is experienced along with the
objective content of that experience.

The philosopher who employs the phenomenological
method will ask the questions: "What is it that
'appears' to man when he experiences a state of consciousness?" "What is it that characterizes a certain type of act, such as 'perceiving,' 'hoping,'
'willing,' 'loving,' 'reasoning'?" "What does the
act of 'religious' consciousness reveal regarding
the object or objects of that act?" "What does the
act of 'moral' consciousness, 'rational' consciousness, or 'aesthetic' consciousness show about the
objects of such acts?" Such acts of consciousness
are not only cognitive, but they may be emotional
as well and be shown to have distinctively different
types of objects. A good example of such a distinction can be found in existential literature between
the emotions of "fear" and "anxiety" (or "dread")
and between objects which correspond to each.[1]
(Anxiety, of course, has no distinct object and thus

remains incurable, whereas fear is always the result of some tangible threat to a man's being, such as a snarling dog, and can be resolved.)

HUSSERL

Edmund Husserl (1859-1938) is without a doubt the central person in the development of the Phenomenological Movement. Even though the whole of Husserl's philosophy is not phenomenological in nature--since it can be shown to have passed through at least three periods of development[2]--his major aim was to make philosophy a strict science.[3] This Husserl hoped to do by a method of description and analysis of consciousness which reflects an effort to resolve the opposition between Empiricism (the Aristolelian emphasis) which stresses observation, and Rationalism (the Platonic emphasis), which stresses a priori reason and theory. It describes and distinguishes the phenomena which is given in consciousness without introducing unverified presuppositions or erroneous deductions.

Despite the fact that Husserl's life-long interests were primarily with logic and the deductive sciences familiar to the mathematician, students of his thought have applied and developed the phenomenological method in the philosophy of language, psychology, the social sciences, and the philosophy of religion. Indeed, disciples of the phenomenological philosophy seem to have caught the wave of the future and investigations have been carried on successfully in a broadening spectrum.[4]

Edmund Husserl was born of Jewish parentage in Prossanitz, a small town in Moravia. He studied in a German public gymnasium in the neighboring city of Olmütz from which he graduated in 1876. After that he went on to study mathematics, physics, astronomy and philosophy in the universities of Leipzig, Berlin, and Vienna. He took his Ph.D. at the University of Vienna in 1882, in the field of mathematics, writing a dissertation entitled "Contributions to the Theory of the Calculus of Variations." For a brief time he studied under the famous theorist of the functions of complex variables, Karl Weierstrass, and held a brief assistantship to Weierstrass while working on his doctorate. From 1884 to 1886 he

attended lectures and studied with a controversial
ex-priest by the name of Franz Brentano, whose "descriptive psychology" obviously had a profound affect
upon Husserl even though Husserl's primary interests
were in the fields of logic and mathematics.[5] It was
Brentano who aroused Husserl's interest in philosophy
and caused him to take up a career in that field at
the University of Halle under a former student of
Brentano's--Carl Stumpf.

Husserl began his teaching career in the year 1887
at the University of Halle as a private lecturer (Pri-
vadozent) where he remained until 1901. He continued
his teaching at Göttingen for the next fifteen years
(1901-1916), and left there to take up a full pro-
fessorship at the University of Frieburg until the
time of his retirement in 1929.

His Methodology

Husserl's philosophy was in process throughout
his entire life, despite certain constant themes by
which it is characterized.[6] Very briefly, for Husserl
phenomenology was an authoritative philosophical
method which he believed would display (1) the certainty and clarity of a pure science while (2) providing the missing "roots," or unverified "presuppositions," for both commonsense and scientific
judgments. It would do this by (3) concentrating
attention upon what actually appears to "immediate
intuition" (the eidetic, the "essential nature" of
things), or focusing upon that which is both certain and basic to the nature of things. The consequences of these strict procedures (4) would expand
the range of consciousness, and thus man's knowledge,
and make clear the inherited biases in those theories
which see the whole of reality in terms of certain
restricted elements of the human experience (such as
naturalism tends to do).[7] The essential thing about
the methodological procedure was to suspend judgment
about the existence or non-existence of the object
present to consciousness ("bracketing") and reduce
it to its primal or most general, universal character--
the "pure" phenomena.[8]

The Man and His Works

Husserl as a person and as a philosopher seemed to be filled with many inward struggles. He was vigorous in asserting his autonomy as a philosopher but still longed for a following among other philosophers. Perhaps this ambivalence of character is best expressed by his agonizing over his own writings. Herbert Spiegelberg notes that the Husserl Archives in Lourain, France, contain some 45,000 pages, written in shorthand, which Husserl produced, intending to publish, but for one reason or another had decided to withhold or withdraw them from publication.[9] Perhaps the classics of his translated works are: <u>Phenomenology and the Crisis of Philosophy</u>; <u>Cartesian Meditations</u>; and <u>The Idea of Phenomenology</u>. However, the book which really furnishes the groundwork for the phenomenological movement is, as translated into English, <u>Ideas: General Introduction to Pure Phenomenology</u>. (Although published in 1913, in Germany, it was not translated and published in English until 1931.)

Before leaving Husserl, a central figure in the phenomenological movement, one aspect of his thought must be mentioned which is of particular interest to the apologetic theologian. There were times when Husserl referred to the functions of the philosopher as a kind of mission which would bring about an ethical "renewal" in society. He saw philosophy as a way of securing greater certainty not only for developing science, but for human development as well. Even though he stressed the importance of the philosopher's autonomy, as well as his responsibility for and to mankind, Husserl also seemed to have certain religious convictions. While he denounced theological dogma, and disclaimed traditional theism, he still expected his phenomenology would eventually aid theological insight. Of course, it should not be forgotten that Husserl was reared in a Jewish home and later became a Protestant. And it was asserted that he had something like a conversion just prior to his death.[10] At any rate, it would appear that Husserl left the door open on the question of God, and his mind most certainly remained open about religious phenomena.

A Variety of Thinkers

"All of phenomenology is not Husserl, even though he is more or less its center."[11] These words spoken by the French philosopher Paul Ricoeur, who is recognized as one of the foremost authorities on the development of the Phenomenological Movement, hint at the great variety among phenomenologists. The phenomenological method has been employed by Heidegger, Sartre, and many other thinkers of the existential and ontological orientation, as well as, by psychologists, philosophers, educators, religionists, and social scientists of increasing diverse interests. It lies both beyond the limits and the purpose of this chapter to look even briefly into the thought of this increasing group of thinkers. However, an attempt will be made to identify several of the key French philosophers whose influence has been of particular importance for phenomenology.

In the early thirties the center of interest in the phenomenological movement shifted from Germany to France with Belgium and the Netherlands becoming secondary advocates.[12] The French became particularly interested in the application of the method in the study of the human body, history, and the social world. Perhaps the real distinctiveness of French phenomenology is its much wider application to a literary expression as opposed to the heavy scholarly style of most German writers who employed the method. Gabriel Marcel consistently combined the roles of philosopher and playwright. Jean-Paul Sartre wrote novels and short stories, plays and screen productions while carrying on his philosophical work. And Jean Wahl included some of his poetry in the same work with his philosophy.[13] Nevertheless, French phenomenology finds its greatest distinctiveness in its close association with existentialism.

One year after his book <u>Being and Nothingness</u> appeared in France, in 1943, Sartre accepted the label "existentialism" which was being applied to him and others who were advocating the philosophy of engagement. At that time the label was consistently rejected by the German scholars Karl Jaspers and Martin Heidegger who had theoretically initiated the concept.[14] Historically, it was Sartre who introduced the French public to phenomenology and who demon-

strated the possibilities of the phenomenological
approach. In the late thirties he was writing critical articles for French scholarly Journals on Husserl,
and his publication of <u>Being and Nothingness</u> presupposes familiarity with German phenomenology--especially
Husserl and Heidegger--and cries out for a comparison
with Heidegger's <u>Being and Time</u>.[15]

Despite the fact that Sartre's phenomenology is
not free from preconceptions, he at least maintains
the principle of the descriptive method based on intuition. And regardless of his rather one-sided and
incomplete understanding of Husserl, it was still
Sartre who revived and aroused an interest in the
founder of phenomenology and, especially, in Husserl's
subjective approach. While Sartre did not recon-
struct phenomenology, or systematize it for the French,
he did naturalize it. It was up to his associates
particularly Maurice Merleau-Ponty (1908-1961), to
give phenomenology deliberate and explicit shape.

The central place which Merleau-Ponty held in
the development of French philosophy is attested to
by his appointment to the chair of philosophy at the
Collège de France in 1952. With this appointment, which
he held until the time of his death, he took his place
as a successor of the great Henry Bergson and Etienne
Gilson. Merleau-Ponty was a native Catholic from La-
Rochelle. He received his basic philosophical education at the École Normale, in Paris, during which
time he became a close friend of Jean-Paul Sartre.
(Over the years this personal friendship became increasingly strained, especially after the outbreak
of the Korean War in 1953, when Sartre's pro-com-
munism seemed to be the last straw.) Up to at least
1950, Merleau-Ponty collaborated closely with Sartre's
magazine <u>Modern Times</u> (<u>Les Temps modernes</u>), but their
philosophical differences became increasingly sharp
and apparently reached a breaking point by 1955.[16]

In 1950 when Merleau-Ponty joined the University
of Sorbonne teaching staff his main assignment was
child psychology. This fact is not without significance since Gestalt psychology was making an increasing impression upon France during this period of history. However, Merleau-Ponty's development as a
phenomenologist had been taking place ever since his
discussions with Sartre who, after returning from

Germany in 1935, had acquainted him with Husserl's
book Ideas. In fact, Merleau-Ponty's book Phénoméno-
logie de la perception (1945), (Phenomenology of perception), was the first systematic work in French to
display the word "phenomenology."[17] In Phenomenology
of Perception, he brought together the most current
developments from the behavioral sciences, Gestalt
psychology, phenomenological studies of Husserl, and
the existential-ontological interpretations of Heidegger and Marcel.[18] It is probably safe to say that
without this significant book French phenomenology
would have remained a tool of existentialism much
longer, as it had increasingly become in the works
of Sartre.

There are several guiding themes which seem to
characterize the philosophy of Merleau-Ponty. The
first theme has to do with the "mysterious" nature
of reason. Man must form a "new idea of reason"
which does not forget the "experience of reason."[19]
For Merleau-Ponty what is real is not completely
rational, just as that which is totally rational is
not completely real. Contingency, the unpredictable,
is just as fundamental in man's experience as is
necessity. Meaning and lack of meaning, reason and
irrationality often appear side by side in life. Indeed, Merleau-Ponty's position has often been called
a philosophy of "ambiguity."[20] This recognition of
the ambiguous nature of reason accounts, in part, for
a second theme found in Merleau-Ponty's thought which
is the absence of final answers or absolutes. This
theme comes out repeatedly in his discussion of "perception" and "freedom."[21]

A third element which persists in Merleau-Ponty's
thought is his existentialism. His philosophy is one
of engagement, commitment, or action. His problem is
that of maintaining a proper balance between engagement,
or "incarnation" within the world, and a detached
perspective which prevents his being completely en-
gulfed by the world. The tension which must be maintained at this point in Merleau-Ponty's life as a
philosopher, or a person, becomes the model for his
phenomenology of perception. The "primacy of perception" is the most basic theme of his entire philosophy, and the phenomenology of perception the key
to his whole endeavor.[22]

Starting with the later Husserl's concept of the world as met in lived experience (<u>Lebenswelt</u>), Merleau-Ponty grounds his phenomenology of perception in this lived, or "incarnated" body which experiences and is experienced. Rather than starting with the "essential nature" of things, the "pure" phenomena, and giving a rigorous objective description of them as the earlier Husserl suggested, Merleau-Ponty begins with the perceiving subject who is the mediating consciousness within the phenomenal world. He then turns his reflection towards the relationship between the world and the perceiver (or subject) to which the phenomena appears. To quote Merleau-Ponty: "I am a thought which recaptures itself as already possessing an ideal of truth (which it cannot at each moment wholly account for) and which is the horizon of its operations."[23] The phenomena which appears to man set the boundaries of everything thinkable or conceivable for him, but the phenomena as phenomena are not open to doubt. Such phenomena are certain and in them there is meaning. The experience of perception is, for Merleau-Ponty, man's presence at the moment in which values, truths, things are constituted for him.[24]

This phenomenology of human "presence within the world," or the existential role of perception, is Merleau-Ponty's endeavor to overcome the rigid dichotomy between the subjective and objective realities as given in human experience, whether they be presented as the opposition between realism and idealism, or empericism and rationalism. While it clearly constitutes the most original feature of Merleau-Ponty's phenomenology, man is still left with some ambiguities. Man is not merely passively involved within the world, but he must be committed to exist! However, this world which he perceives is only partly given, and only partly of man's own making through perception, since man depends upon his "incarnation" in a pre-given world. He is nothing but a certain perspective of the world and a very finite perspective at that. These ambiguities and relativities which Merleau-Ponty's phenomenology of perception uncover are helpful to the understanding of the anthropological sciences (in which he was very interested), but would appear to be self-defeating for the natural sciences.

For Merleau-Ponty the phenomenology of perception is basically an endeavor to lay bare the primary

stratum in the human experience of the world as it is
given prior to all scientific or philosophical distortions. But the question may be asked, "How is
phenomenology still possible when it no longer can
detach itself from its involvement in the phenomena?"
How far does "engagement" in the body and in history
allow man to look upon his own consciousness with the
necessary distance? Does not the identification of
existence and body come dangerously close to selling
the birthright of phenomenology? It is precisely
this phenomenology of insertion into a field of perception, action, and living--a phenomenology of
"finitude"--which points up Paul Ricoeur's differences
with Merleau-Ponty.

RICOEUR - Philosopher-Theologian

Paul Ricoeur (1913-   ) asserts that the experience of finitude presents itself paradoxically.
The experience of "being-in-the-world" presents itself as a dual, or contrasting experience of both
"limitation" and "transgression."[25] Consequently,
the experience must not be described in two separate
stages, as Merleau-Ponty does, but as it is in its
duality. It is a mistake to work out a description
of man's being present in the world in "perception"
and, then, proceed to initiate his "transcendence"
of his presence in the world by the "word" or the
"will." On the contrary, man's experience of "being-
in-the-world" presents itself simultaneously as the
act of embodiment and the transcending of embodiment.[26] Man's point of view and man's perspective
are known as such by man's power to constantly transcend them. "How can I know my perspective as perspective in the very act of perceiving if I did not
somehow escape it? It is this 'somehow' which constitutes the essence of the whole question."[27] It
is man's "word," the very possibility of "saying,"
the "meaning-giving act" which reveals the transcendence, so that the dialectic of signifying and perceiving appear as absolutely primal for Ricoeur.[28]

Ricoeur, perhaps more than any other philosopher
today, has excited theologians about the possibilities of a phenomenological theology.[29] Ricoeur was
born in Valence, France, and is the son of Protestant
parents. He took his <u>Docteur</u> <u>es</u> <u>Lettres</u> from the
University of Paris in philosophy. He was professor

of philosophy at the University of Strasbourg from
1948-57, then moved to the Sorbonne, University of
Paris. While still considered a professor of general
philosophy at the Sorbonne, in 1971 Ricoeur became a
professor of philosophy at the University of Chicago.
He also became John Nuveen Professor in the Divinity
School at the University of Chicago, a chair first
held by the great Paul Tillich (in 1962), the specific
purpose of which is to relate religion to life.
(Ricoeur has now, apparently, returned to France for
the remainder of his academic career.)

In his early career as a scholar Ricoeur was
exposed to the theology of Karl Barth but was repel-
led by it. He singles out the thought of Gabriel
Marcel as the "decisive philosophical shock" in his
life, but he has been greatly influenced by numerous
other philosophers as well. Although Ricoeur is
recognized as probably the best informed, most original and creative of the French phenomenologists,
phenomenology for him is only the beginning of philosophy.[30] In his thought and life Ricoeur has been
primarily interested in political and moral issues,
as well as philosophical issues. As a man rooted in
the faith of the Reformation he has been a strong
supporter of the ecumenical movement and a "listener
to the Christian message." Perhaps most of all he
has been a man of dialogue and draws upon the sources
of sociology, philosophy, political theory, and theology as a means of continuing meaningful dialogue.[31]
Spiegelberg declares that Ricoeur's philosophical goal
is to develop a philosophy which unites a sense of the
mysterious with clear understanding.[32]

While there are many important distinctions which
have been made regarding the relationship of Ricoeur
to Husserl, Merleau-Ponty, Sartre, Marcel, and others,
in various aspects of the phenomenological development, the primary concern here is with Ricoeur's philosophical developments which seem particularly important for the apologetic theologian. In contrast
to Sartre's philosophy of despair, Ricoeur has developed a philosophy of optimism. While in most re-
spects he is more faithful to the rigorous "descriptive" phenomenology of Husserl's early conception,
and accepts Husserl's view that "consciousness" is
not empty but always directed toward an object ("in-
tentional"), he rejects Husserl's notion of "transcendental" idealism.[33]

151

Man - a Broken Unity

Ricoeur's most systematic and significant work has been in the area of the phenomenology of the will. Philosophy of the Will is a monumental work which will eventually appear as a three volume creation with several sub-parts.[34] One of Ricoeur's basic endeavors is to provide a description of the human volition which will show its potential both for innocence and for meriting condemnation--man is a broken unity. His phenomenology of finitude makes clear the underlying structures of man's dual nature as innocent and culpable, as voluntary and involuntary, as transcending finitude and limited by finitude.

Ricoeur's Philosophy of the Will is an endeavor to establish the reciprocal relationship between the voluntary and involuntary in the human experience. It is the endeavor to integrate the notions of "body" and "consciousness" of man into a whole rather than separate them into two distinct parts. He, therefore, rejects the kind of determinism found in empirical psychology which treats consciousness as another "object" which can be studied quantitatively. But he, also, rejects the kind of transcendental ego-- found in Husserl--which ignores the dual nature of man. According to Ricoeur, every bodily state has a corresponding subjective consciousness. And the acts of volition by man can only be comprehended as "intentions" which are actualized by means of the body as an object in the world. He insists upon the recognition of a dynamic interplay between voluntary and involuntary aspects of incarnate existence. It is not possible to explain either the physical or the subjective aspects of bodily existence solely in terms of the other. Consequently, the will of man is free but not completely free. For Ricoeur, man has a "bound-freedom," a freedom which is limited by all the determinate aspects of the body.[35]

A Description of the Human Will

Ricoeur offers an eidetic description (a description of the essential structures) of human volition. However, in order to make clear man's possibilities two aspects of his situation must be postponed ("bracketed") until the essential struc-

tures of human volition have been clarified. These
two aspects are the "fault" (the condition in which
man appears to be ruled by a perverted will) and
"transcendence" (the ontological basis of subjectivity). Both notions must be bracketed because they
are inextricably linked, according to Ricoeur. The
"fault" refers to all those defects or ruptures in
man's nature, the brokenness of human existence. The
experience of the fault in the presence of God is the
experience of "sin." The transcendence, when understood as Being, transforms the experience of the fault
into alienation. However, Ricoeur insists that
neither of these two notions can be investigated by
means of _eidetic_ analysis and that a new descriptive
method and means of interpretation must be developed.[36]

While a philosophical anthropology can inquire
into the occasion for evil by discovering the dynamic
interplay of the voluntary and involuntary within
incarnate existence, and man's "bound-freedom," the
reality of evil is always expressed in terms of myths
and symbols. Therefore, after Ricoeur had made clear
the possibility of man's flawed, disproportionate
structure in the first part of his second volume,
Fallible Man, he went on in the second part, _The Symbolism of Evil_, to attempt a hermeneutics of this
flawed nature as expressed in images, myths, and
symbols.[37] Ricoeur's progressive development of a
hermeneutical phenomenology of religious and symbolic
language is proving to be the most creative aspect
of his work. Indeed, his continuation of the development of this method of interpretation may ultimately serve the purpose of making him the greatest
philosophical theologian of this era! Briefly, what
is his interpretative approach?

His Interpretative Method

The first task of a hermeneutic, according to
Ricoeur, is to identify those "originary modes of discourse through which the religious faith of a community comes to language."[38] The most primitive expressions of a community of faith are, says Ricoeur,
those through which the members of a community interpret their experiences for their own sake or for
the sake of others. These expressions of faith are
not basically theological statements of a metaphysical
nature, but expressions which are embedded in such

forms of language as hymns, prayers, proverbs and wisdom sayings, legislative texts, prophecies, and narratives. The philosophical hermeneutics must provide methodological tools which will clarify the idea of the "modes," or forms, of such discourse. For instance, it will note the relation between the speech, as an act, and its content, because this relation implies something about the "most primitive dialectics" of objectification upon which the different forms of discourse develop into literary forms. Not only is there a "distance" between what is said and the act of saying it, but a similar "distance may be noticed between the discourse and its speaker, the inner structure and the outer referent, the discourse and its initial situation, and the discourse and its first audience."[39] Hence, the complex dialectics of oral language itself, which provides the basis for the forms of "discourse," creates the problem of interpretation even before it gets written down in a definite form.

Ricoeur points out that the "modes of discourse"-- narratives, proverbs, poems, and so forth--are more than just a way of classifying literature. They are a means of creating a "work" and, as such, are organized into "wholes" of a higher order. The sentence is the minimal unit for discourse. The understanding of a text, whether oral or written, is always something much more than an analysis of its parts because it presents a "texture" and demands an interpretation of its inner structure. Discourse as a "work," like a work of art, takes on an additional kind of "distance" opening up an infinite number of problems for interpretation. As a "work" it becomes autonomous, an object, separated not only from its author, but the situation in life which gave it birth and the primitive audience to whom it was addressed. To recover the initial event of the discourse a form of reconstruction, or interpretation, must proceed from the inner organization of the specific modes of the discourse. This means that in order to recover the initial event of the discourse in a revitalized way, which is both faithful and creative, hermeneutics must not only overcome distance (as an obstacle) but use it (as the instrument).[40]

If the philosophical interpreter accepts Ricoeur's first thesis--namely that the religious faith of a com-

munity must be uncovered through its specific modes
of language--then he is prepared to understand the
second thesis. The second thesis asserts that the
meanings of religious language "are ruled and guided
by the modes of articulation specific to each mode of
discourse."[41] In the biblical documents, for example,
the "confession of faith" which is expressed there
is peculiar to the "forms of discourse"--the narrative structure of parables, Pentateuch and Gospels,
the oracular structure of the prophetic literature,
and so forth--found in the Bible. Not just any
theology can be tied into the narrative forms of the
Old Testament which proclaim that the grand Actor on
the stage of history, the great Deliverer, is Jahweh.
The confessions of faith found in the various modes
of discourse in the Old Testament are homogeneous
with the narrative structure itself.[42]

Ricoeur's third thesis is perhaps the most daring
and creative in his theory of interpretation. Briefly
stated it declares that religious language "develops
specific claims to truth measured by criteria appropriate to this kind of discourse."[43] The question
is: "What happens to the reference (the claim to
reach or touch truth, or reality) in discourse when
it becomes a text?" In oral discourse the "reference"
is resolved by the power of the speaker to demonstrate
the validity of his point of view to the others involved in the dialogue. However, with written discourse there is no longer a common situation existing
between author and reader and every reference to the
given reality may be destroyed. In fact it seems to
be the role of most literature to do just that--to
destroy this world. Here Ricoeur calls attention to
fictional literature--fairy tales, myths, novels,
drama--but also to all that literature entitled "poetic"
literature.[44] Indeed, Ricoeur points out that poetic
language seems to glorify itself without depending on
the reality function of ordinary language.

Nevertheless, Ricoeur notes that while fictional
and poetic discourse do not reply to ordinary reality,
they still speak to an even more basic level of reality, or truth, than that attained by assertive, didac-
tic, or descriptive discourse (that is, "ordinary"
language). Ricoeur's thesis is, therefore, that the
destruction of ordinary language (what he calls "first-
order reference")--as accomplished by fiction and

poetry--provides the possibility for the liberation
of language at a more basic level (what he calls a
"second-order of reference").[45] This "second-order
of reference" is that way of perceiving reality as
it is "unfolded in front of the text;" it is a mode
of being-in-the-world in the Heideggerian sense (as
that being who is always on its way). For Ricoeur
hermeneutics must go beyond a mere identification of
the structures of discourse, or a searching out of
the person or the psychological intentions hidden
behind the text. It must identify the deeper level
of truth or reality.

The world of the text of which Ricoeur speaks
is not the world of ordinary or everyday discourse.
Rather, it comprises a new sort of distance of the
real from itself. It is the distance which fiction,
poetry, or a fairy tale introduces into man's understanding of reality. Such literary discourse does
not lack a truth claim (a "referent"), rather it introduces a "second-order" referent or "new possibilities of being-in-the-world." Thus, while fiction
and poetry intend to depict a reality, or state of
being, it is not through the modes as given, but
rather through the modes of possibility. "And in this
way everyday reality is metamorphosed by means of
what we call the imaginative variations that literature works on the real."[46]

Religious Texts Are Kinds of Poetic Texts

This understanding of the world of the text leads
Ricoeur to assert that religious texts are "kinds of
poetic texts." By this he means that biblical texts,
for instance, present "modes of redescribing life."
However, they do this in a manner which differentiates
them from other forms of poetic texts.[47] This hermeneutic of poetic texts, as applied to biblical texts,
not only restores biblical interpretation to its own
laws of interpretation but prevents it from falling
into certain illusions. Ricoeur gives four examples
that seem pertinent.

First of all, the phenomenological hermeneutic
unfolds the "objective" realities of the text, the
world of the text, before considering the theological
implications of the text. The first task of the interpreter is to allow the world of being to unfold

before the text above and beyond belief, or non-belief, emotions, or disposition. This, for Ricoeur, means that the interpreter is delivered from the temptation of any premature existential categories for understanding the notions of a new world, a new birth, a new covenant, and the kingdom of God.[48]

A second implication of this approach is that by putting the issue of the text before everything else the revelatory nature of the biblical world, if such is present, is not inflated by the projections of the interpreter. "Revelation, if the expression is meaningful, is a trait of the biblical world."[49] It is not something added. It must be mediated through the structures of the texts themselves, since the immediate psychological intentions are not open to the interpreter.

A third theological implication mentioned by Ricoeur concerns the global horizon of the world of the text. Because the biblical text concerns a world of a totality of meanings, there is no prerogative for instructions spoken to the individual person. Man is addressed through a multiplicity of dimensions in the biblical world--the cosmic (concerning creation), the communitarian (the people of God), the historical and cultural, and the personal.[50]

Finally, since the world of the religious text is a projected world which is "poetically distant" from the ordinary world of reality, Ricoeur suggests that man must accord to it the "poetic dimension."[51] Which means that the "new being" projected and proposed by the Bible makes its presence known through the world of ordinary experience in spite of the end of that original experience. Through the "poetic dimension" what is opened up in everyday reality is another reality--the reality of the "possible." The "new being," the "kingdom of God" as coming, which appeals to man's utmost possibilities.

Ricoeur contends that this general hermeneutical approach when applied to the biblical hermeneutic is the only route which will make the biblical "issue" specific and disclose it as Word of God.[52] But he warns once again that this recognition is addressed to the "quality of the new being" as it presents itself and not to some psychological notion of inspiration.

Two Traits Which Illustrate His Point

Ricoeur takes two traits concerning the specificity in biblical discourse to illustrate this hermeneutical approach. The first is the central place which "God-talk" holds in biblical discourse. The term "God" does not function as a philosophical concept in the Bible, but as a word which says much more. In order to understand the word "God" in biblical discourse the interpreter must follow the "direction of its meaning." By this Ricoeur means its "double power to gather all the significations which issue from the partial discourses and to open up a horizon which escapes from the closure of discourse."[53] While the term "God" coordinates all the varied signs, symbols, and statements about Him in the biblical literature, it also points to the incompleteness of all such discourse.

The second example which he indicates points to the specific focus in biblical discourse is the word "Christ." This word, in addition to the double function which Ricoeur attributes to the word "God," gathers all the religious signs into a fundamental symbol. This is the symbol of a "sacrificial love, of a love stronger than death."[54] It is, of course, the task of biblical hermeneutics to pursue all the implications of this manner of speaking about God.

The phenomenological method has developed a number of techniques, such as intuiting, analyzing, describing, suspending judgment ("bracketing"), watching the modes of appearance (viewing objects or entities from different perspectives), investigating general essences (illustrated by the pure color which lies behind the various shades within a spectrum), apprehending essential relationships between several essences or within a single essence, but in general the phenomenological method can be described as a protest against uncritical simplifications.[55] More specifically, it is a protest against the reductionist approach whether it be in science or philosophy. However, the phenomenological hermeneutic is forced to go beyond those meanings which may be more immediately given by intuiting, analyzing, and describing. In endeavoring to do this, the interpreter has to use the "given" as a clue for meanings which are not explicitly given. While this task of unveiling

hidden meanings will, naturally, always remain to some
degree ambiguous, the apologetic theologian, like the
philosopher, must take the risk and seek for clarification.

An Apologetic Future?

Although the phenomenological method has long
been employed by the historian of religion, the
scholars of comparative religions and the philosopher
of religion,[56] the theologian has been hesitant in
his endeavor to work out a phenomenological hermeneutic. And those who have made an endeavor in this
direction have met with limited success for one reason
or another. Two theologians, whose books called considerable attention to the possibilities of a phenomenological hermeneutic in the late sixties, are Thomas
Oden and Langdon Gilkey.

ODEN

Oden, the younger of the two, received his Ph.D.
from Yale in 1960, and teaches in the Department of
Theology at Drew University, Madison, New Jersey.
His book The Structure of Awareness (1969) represents
a departure from his earlier scholarly efforts to
bridge the gap between the disciplines of psycho-
therapy and theology.[57] His highly imaginative description of the "structures of awareness" (which
was his phrase for Husserl's notion of the intuitive
essence of experience)[58] has contributed to the growing interest in the phenomenological method. His
thesis contends that human awareness develops directly
out of the three modes of temporal consciousness (past,
present, and future) and the relationship to the four
modes of being (God, self, neighbor, and the world).[59]
In the first three chapters of his book, Oden describes
the fall of the human organism from its newborn innocence to a state of guilt. The newborn's situation in
the world is then considered as a prototype of man's
primordial relationship to reality. The question is:
How is man to recover his neonate innocence? At this
point Oden jumps abruptly to a biblically based ontology of revelation.[60] Thus the major problem with
Oden's endeavor to do phenomenological hermeneutics
is his methodology. To begin with a theologically
neutral description of the life-world implies that
such an ontology has relevance somehow for the con-

tent of the received faith. However, Oden fails to demonstrate this because he moves immediately into a description of a "covenant ontology" based on God's self-disclosure in Christ.

GILKEY

Langdon Gilkey's book <u>Naming the Whirlwind: The Renewal of God-Language</u> (1969) is an extended critical introduction to theological discourse which endeavors to establish the meaningfulness of religious discourse in general as related to human existence. Gilkey calls this endeavor "an ontic prolegomenon" to theological language.[61] He explicitly notes the importance of the hermeneutical techniques developed by phenomenology for this undertaking.[62] Gilkey, a distinguished graduate of Union Theological Seminary (New York) and Columbia University (Ph.D., 1954), a former recipient of a Fulbright Scholarship to Cambridge and Guggenheim fellowships to both Germany and Rome, is well qualified as a theologian. Currently Professor of Theology at The Divinity School, The University of Chicago, Gilkey has written a penetrating, insightful analysis of the current dilemma of theology.

In <u>Naming the Whirlwind</u> Gilkey endeavors to analyze the collapse of "God-language," which had become so apparent in the 1960's, and to offer a rationale for its renewal. This renewal is based on an analysis of the modern secular experience itself. This experience which Gilkey sees as characterized by the dissolution of all absolutes, creates an environment for man of relativity, transiency, dependency and autonomy.[63] Within a pluralism of so many possible authorities man in his autonomy determines all questions of value and meaning and declares religious discourse to be "unintelligible." However, what the secular man does not understand, according to Gilkey, is that he is experiencing the very same aspects of human finitude to which religious language has previously spoken.[64] What then is to be done for secular contemporary man?

Very much reminiscent of Paul Tillich's method of correlation, in which existential questions of man are correlated with theological answers, Gilkey asserts that questions raised by ordinary secular experience can be answered by the Christian message about the sacred dimension of life.[65] The answers seem to hinge upon whether or not the theologian can make clear to secular man the "symbolic" nature of all religious language, especially that language concerning man's ultimate concern. For Gilkey the Christian awareness of God develops out of "the wonder and the ambiguity" of everyday human experience in the world. Man's initial experience of faith grows out of the encounter of the "Void" (the negativities of despair, insecurity, guilt and death).[66] It is this "Void" when interpreted symbolically in the light of religious tradition, Biblical and historical, that faith in "God" is born. This interpretation must be worked out with the tools of "eidetic phenomenology," according to Gilkey, and complemented with a "hermeneutical phenomenology" which deals with the secular experiences of people today.[67] Unfortunately, Gilkey's insightful and penetrating analysis of the theological dilemma has not led him to develop a sufficiently clear procedural methodology for a convincing apologetic theology. After 470 pages Gilkey still has only a "prolegomenon"--a preface, an introduction-- to a phenomenological hermeneutic.

Before looking at one further attempt to do phenomenological theology, a brief comment seems to be in order concerning the application of phenomenology to the study of religion in general.

SMART

Ninian Smart, a Professor of Religious Studies at the University of Lancaster, Lancaster, England, is a distinguished scholar of the history of religion and the philosophy of religion and the author of numerous books on both subjects. In a recent book, The Phenomenon of Religion (1973), Smart makes some interesting observations on the distinction between the study of Religion and the study of Theology. He declares that the study of religion must be undertaken with "empathetic objectivity" or "neutralist subjectivity" if it is to succeed in uncovering the richness of religion in man's experience.[68] For Smart, phenomenology must do more than just give a description of the religious experience while at the same time it must guard against doing theology. Theo-

161

logy is basically evocative ("Expressive"), it expresses a world-view and leads to a "commitment" to that world-view.[69] But the description of the religious life as undertaken by the phenomenologist of religion must not cut off a sensitive understanding of such a life if he is to be faithful to his task. Following the suggestion of Mircea Eliade, Smart contends that the Religionist must allow for a "creative hermeneutic."[70] This means that if the student of religion is successful in his endeavor to present his subject matter he must present a "sympathetic objective awareness" of the various religious faiths. If successful, this creates an "internalized consciousness" of the richness of symbols, beliefs, values, feelings, and ritual.[71]

According to Smart, the phenomenologist as such is not committed to mere indifference, agnosticism, or what have you, any more than he is committed to a particular religious world-view.[72] The Religionist should enter into the "feel" of the values and truths of that which he is examining. For this reason Smart uses the term "empathy" because it expresses the effective side of the Religionist's study--the entering into the world of another but without the same commitment. The phenomenologist should make use of "empathetic imagination." Empathetic imagination involves a "bracketing" of attitudes and feelings in the researcher himself. Smart suggests two models for the doing of religion phenomenologically--that which is demanded of an actor who must act out a variety of attitudes and feelings, and the sympathetic imagination necessary in learning a new language.[73] It appears that Smart's phenomenological method endeavors to walk a fine line between religion as an empirical study and theology as the study of the focus through which a particular faith is given expression--the fine line between ecstatic participation and reductive detachment.

VOGEL

One further attempt at phenomenological theology must be considered before concluding this account of what is obviously the frontier of apologetic theology today. It is the work of Bishop Arthur A. Vogel, a former Sub-Dean and Professor of Philosophical and Systematic Theology at Nashotah House Theological

Seminary, Nashotah, Wisconsin. Bishop Vogel, who received a Ph.D. from Harvard University in 1952, is presently Bishop of the Episcopal Diocese of the western Missouri Episcopal Church. Despite the fact that Vogel is a member of the American Philosophical Society, and several other learned, philosophical organizations, his use of phenomenology and philosophy is not critical. His most recent and comprehensive appropriation of philosophical phenomenology appears in his book Body Theology: God's Presence in Man's World (1973).

Vogel's approach is simply an appropriation of what he calls "secular insights" as a means of making clear the "experiential," and therefore, bodily basis of man's knowledge of God. He insists that since man is a "person" he must have a religion that is as personal as he himself is.[74] To think of God as somehow impersonal being or power is to Vogel the height of naivete. Although Vogel declares that "reality" is basic to the consolation of man in the world and that people must live with it, he never indicates what precisely "reality" is except that man's body locates him in it.[75] However, he then proceeds to assert that man is "more than" a bodily location, and, indeed, that he transcends his body through "personal presence."[76] Where this leaves the matter of "reality" is not quite clear.

"Personal presence" becomes the key to understanding Vogel's Body Theology. He begins with the assertion that man knows the objective world because he, himself, is a body.[77] He proceeds to argue that while there are no absolute differences among physical entities in the universe, yet man's "consciousness" separates him from other physical things as well as from other men. When the focus on man is shifted from the "how" of his location in the world to the "what" is located, Vogel asserts that it becomes clear the manner in which man goes beyond his body in "personal presence."[78] Vogel borrows from the thought of the French phenomenologist Emmanual Levinas the notion that personal presence implies the "infinity" of man (which appears to be an expansion of the notion of man's self-transcendence). "Personal presence" is a way of referring to that which "overflows thought," that which cannot be systematically or completely accounted for, or summed up, in a person. It refers to the absolute "otherness," the more of a person which prohibits his being reduced to a mere object. According to Vogel it is not an abstract idea but is a kind of "being," an immediate experience of the "infinite" which makes possible man's awareness (not intellectual understanding) of his own "infinitude."[79] "Personal presence" is too much for thought alone to deal with, according to Vogel, and makes man "wonder" about himself. At the same time, "personal presence" provides the basis for man's positive experience of yearning for God.

Vogel declares that man lives by meaning. However, most men have trouble accounting for the source of meaning--that which limits chaos and anarchy, that which prohibits the arbitrary. Meaning originates, says Vogel, within the context of a Gestalt (figure-ground relationship), or a wholelistic view in which particulars fit into a larger context. The human being as a particular perspective, or location in the world, finds meaning only where some sense of orderliness prevails. That which is indecisive and arbitrary destroys man's sense of security and meaning. Vogel contends, therefore, that the only entity that can really satisfy this longing for meaning is that which is inexhaustible or ultimate. The immediate encounter of such a source is in another person, or "personal presence."[80]

Actually, it is through language, or speaking, that "personal presence" manifests its inexhaustible character. The presence of another person can challenge and question a man's very being. The person elicits meaning from another precisely because he is recognized as a source of meaning himself. While meaning speaks to man, the ultimate importance of speech is that the speaker remains present in his words as interpreter. The speaker is the inexhaustible location who stands behind his words and as an unlimited source of activity cannot be reduced to his mere external body. Indeed, his words are an extension of his body, and "meaning" is found in his words as he is found in his body.[81] His words are embodied presence and, at the same time, he overflows them and is much more than they can contain. Thus, while personal presence is more than words, man is able to know this only through his words.

According to Vogel as man matures the meaning which he found adequate in the presence of primary family relationships, as a child, no longer appears adequate to the reality which confronts him. Death and the age and extent of the physical universe surpass man's resources. In these circumstances man realizes that if his life is to have any final meaning it must live in a "presence" which can explain the totality of the universe and be capable of transcending death. Hence, says Vogel, man is led to the recognition that he needs "a presence" which is the basis of all reality. Man is led to recognize his need of "God."[82]

Very briefly, Body Theology is a description of man as "personal presence" whose nature is to be a "body-word." Man has a choice as to what he says as body-word. Man's need for meaning exceeds that which he discovers in human presence and this leads him to recognize the need for an "Other" whose "presence" provides meaning for the whole universe. Presence can only be recognized by presence. It takes "infinitude" to recognize "infinitude." Although God as Personal Presence is absolutely different from men, as Source of all meaning God is nevertheless present as he is present within the Church which is His "project," activity or body expression in the world.[83] Christ, says Vogel, is the fulfillment of man as a body-word in the world. His Word is the "exteriorization" of God's Presence. By identifying themselves in time with Christ, Christians become the presence of his lived body, his life style in the world.

It is difficult to assign any value to Vogel's work in terms of apologetic theology. While he has appropriated many of the concepts which some of the phenomenologists use, he does not proceed in a critical or systematic interpretation of these concepts. Rather, his approach is more that of a pastoral approach which encourages Christians to sense the reality of God in some mystical or bodily experience. Body Theology is not directed to the intellectual skeptics either within the faith or outside the faith. Perhaps its value lies in the notion that phenomenological terminology has become popular!

It is not yet clear whether phenomenological theology will rally a new generation of supporters

of the caliber of those who have invested their
talents in the development of process and existential theologies. The history of apologetic theology
would seem to indicate that two criteria are necessary before such a development takes place. First,
the philosophical position must become widely accepted. As has been indicated, both in this chapter
and in the previous chapter, phenomenological methodology has been used in an ever increasing number of
disciplines and is undergoing continuing refinements.
Perhaps the most hopeful refinements taking place
within the method itself are those leading to a general theory of interpretation of discourse (a hermeneutic phenomenology), and the kinds of scholarly
refinements that are taking place in the study of
religion in general (as illustrated by Ninian Smart).
A second criterion is the appearance of a truly
creative theologian or philosopher who appropriates
and applies the philosophy in a convincing manner.
At this point in time the most likely candidate
would appear to be Paul Ricoeur. But only time will
determine this.

¹See, for instance, Quentin Lauer, S. J., "Phenomenology as Resource for Christian Thinking," in Philosophical Resources for Christian Thought, edited by Perry LeFevre (Abingdon Press, 1968), p. 73.

²Without a doubt the best history of the phenomenological movement is the two volume work of Herbert Spiegelberg, The Phenomenological Movement: A Historical Introduction (2 ed.; The Hague: Martinus Nijhoff, 1965), 2 vols. See Vol. I, p. 74, for a discussion of the various periodizations of Husserl's philosophical development. This author remains much indebted to Spiegelberg's interpretation of phenomenology.

³Cf. John Macquarrie, Twentieth-Century Religious Thought: The Frontiers of Philosophy and Theology, 1900-1960 (Harper and Row, 1963), p. 218.

⁴Quentin Lauer, for example, notes the successful application of this type of investigation in the areas of the "will" by Paul Ricoeur, the "imagination" by Jean-Paul Sartre, in the areas of "aesthetic response" by George Simmel, "social consciousness" by Edith Stein, "perception" by Maurice Merleau-Ponty, "hope" by Gabriel Marcel, "artistic creativity" by Andre Malraux, "moral consciousness" by Dietrich von Hildebrand, and, of course, Max Scheler in the realm of "religious consciousness." See Lauer, op. cit., pp. 73-74. Cf. also the numerous applications of phenomenology in Readings in Existential Phenomenology, edited by Nathaniel Lawrence and Daniel O'Connor (Prentice-Hall, Inc., 1967); also, see Paul Ricoeur, Husserl: An Analysis of His Phenomenology, trans. by Edward G. Ballard and Lester E. Embree (Northwestern University Press, 1967), p. 4.

⁵For a history of Brentano and his influence upon Husserl and the Phenomenological Movement see Spiegelberg, op. cit., vol. I, pp. 27-50; 92.

⁶See ibid., pp. 75-91.

⁷Cf. ibid.; also, Vol. II, 656-658; see also Langdon Gilkey, Naming the Whirlwind: The Renewal of God-Language (The Bobbs-Merril Company, 1969), pp. 242-243, and notes 8, 9, and 10.

⁸See Edmund Husserl, Ideas: General Introduction to Pure Phenomenology, translated by W. R. Boyce Gibson (Collier Books, 1962), pp. 72-73; 75-76; 78; 83.

[9]See Spiegelberg, op. cit., vol. 1, pp. 88-91, for further discussion about the complexities of Husserl's personality.

[10]Cf. Spiegelberg, ibid., pp. 84-87.

[11]Paul Ricoeur, op. cit., p. 3.

[12]See Spiegelberg, op. cit., vol. II, p. 395.

[13]See ibid., pp. 415-418.

[14]See Spiegelberg's discussion of "Phenomenology and Existentialism" ibid., pp. 408-413. The term "existentialism," according to Spiegelberg, is not used in Sartre's Being and Nothingness (L'Être et le néaut) and he protested its application to his philosophy initially. However, Sartre's best known expression of existentialism comes in his later work in a lecture entitled "Existentialism is a Humanism" which was published in 1946. (L'Existentialisme est un Humanisme) See Spiegelberg, ibid., pp. 473-476.

[15]See ibid., pp. 446-447; 449-455; 467-469.

[16]For further discussion on these personal and philosophical differences see ibid., pp. 518-524.

[17]See ibid., p. 516.

[18]Cf. the "Translators' Introduction" in Maurice Merleau-Ponty, Sense and Non-Sense, trans. by H. L. Dreyfus and P. A. Dreyfus (Northwestern University Press, 1964), pp. x-xi.

[19]See Merleau-Ponty, Sense and Non-Sense, pp. 3-4. Cf. also his Phenomenology of Perception, trans. by Colin Smith (Routledge and Kegan Paul, 1962), pp. xxi.

[20]Cf. Spiegelberg's discussion of the work of Ferdinand Alquie and Alphonse de Waelheus, op. cit., vol. II, pp. 526, 539, 523.

[21]Cf. ibid., pp. 526, 544 ff, 553 ff; see also Merleau-Ponty, Phenomenology of Perception, pp. 203 ff, et passim; 434 ff.

[22]In the book by Maurice Merleau-Ponty, The Primacy of Perception: And Other Essays on Phenomenological Psychology, the Philosophy of Art, History and Politics, edited by James M. Edie (Northwestern University Press, 1964), chapter 2 entitled "The Primacy of Perception and Its Philosophical Consequences," Merleau-Ponty gives his general philosophical position as elaborated in his work Phenomenology of Perception. This chapter is very important because it sets forth the underlying thesis of "perception" in its most concise form.

[23]Ibid., p. 22.

[24]Cf. ibid., p. 25.

[25]See Paul Ricoeur, <u>History and Truth</u>, trans. by Charles A. Kelbley (Northwestern University Press, 1965), pp. 306-311.

[26]See <u>ibid.</u>, p. 306.

[27]<u>Ibid.</u>, p. 308.

[28]See <u>ibid.</u>, pp. 308-309; 327.

[29]See, for example, the excellent article by David Tracy, "The Task of Fundamental Theology," <u>The Journal of Religion</u>, Vol. 54, No. 1 (January, 1974), 13-34, in which he outlines a model for contemporary theology based upon the phenomenological method drawing heavily upon the thought of Ricoeur. This model and method for doing theology is worked out in detail by Tracy in a book published by Seabury Press in 1975, entitled <u>A Blessed Rage for Order: The New Pluralism in Theology</u>. Tracy has contributed an article to the current series of "New Turns in Religious Thought" published in the <u>Christian Century</u> (March 19, 1975), 280-284, under the title "Theology as Public Discourse" in which he, once again, calls attention to the significant work of Paul Ricoeur in linguistic and phenomenological analysis of religious language. See <u>loc. cit.</u>, p. 282. Another author who has employed a phenomenological method is Edward Farley, <u>Ecclesial Man: A Social Phenomenology of Faith and Reality</u>, a 1975 publication by Fortress Press.

[30]See Spiegelberg, <u>op. cit.</u>, vol. II, pp. 563-564.

[31]Cf. David Stewart, "The Christian and Politics: Reflections on Power in the Thought of Paul Ricoeur." <u>The Journal of Religion</u>, Vol. 52, No. 1 (January, 1972), 56-57; also, Spiegelberg, <u>op. cit.</u>, vol. II, pp. 568-69.

[32]See <u>op. cit.</u>, vol. II, p. 569; Cf. Ricoeur, <u>op. cit.</u>, p. xvii.

[33]See Ricoeur, <u>Freedom and Nature: The Voluntary and the Involuntary</u> (Northwestern University Press, 1966), p. 14, Cf. Steward, <u>loc. cit.</u>, 70-71.

[34]Vol. I is <u>The Voluntary and the Involuntary</u>; vol. 2 is <u>Finitude and Guilt</u> which appears as two separate books, Part 1, as <u>Fallible Man</u>, Part 2 as <u>Symbolism of Evil</u>. The third volume is entitled <u>Poetics of the Will</u>.

[35]See Stewart, <u>loc. cit.</u>, 72-73; also, Ricoeur, <u>History and Truth</u>, pp. xvi-xvii; 306-311; 327; <u>Freedom and Nature</u>, pp. 68f.

[36]Cf. Stewart, <u>loc. cit.</u>, 71-72; also, Ricoeur, <u>Freedom and Nature</u>, pp. 14, 29.

[37]These two books are available as _Fallible Man_ (Chicago: Henry Regnery Co., 1965); _Symbolism of Evil_ (New York: Harper & Row, 1967).

[38]Ricoeur, "Philosophy and Religious Language," _The Journal of Religion_, Vol. 54, No. 1 (January, 1974), p. 73.

[39]_Ibid._, p. 74.

[40]See _ibid._, p. 74-75.

[41]_Ibid._, p. 75.

[42]See _ibid._, 76-78.

[43]_Ibid._, p. 78.

[44]See _ibid._, p. 79.

[45]See _ibid._, 79-80. Cf. the remarks and, especially, notes 36, 37, 39, of David Tracy's article, "The Task of Fundamental Theology," _loc. cit._, p. 26-27.

[46]Ricoeur, _ibid._, p. 80.

[47]See _ibid._

[48]See _ibid._, p. 81.

[49]_Ibid._

[50]See _ibid._, p. 81-82.

[51]See _ibid._, p. 82.

[52]See _ibid._

[53]_Ibid._, p. 83.

[54]_Ibid._

[55]See Spiegelberg, _op. cit._, vol. II, chapter XIV, for an excellent summary of "the essentials of the phenomenological method."

[56]For example, Rudolf Otto's _The Idea of the Holy_ was first published in 1917 (_Das Heilige_, Breslau, 19-17); Van der Leeuw's _Religion in Essence and Manifestation_ was first published in 1933 (_Phänomenologie der Religion_, Tübingen, 1933); and Jean Hering's _Phénoménologie et philosophie religieuse_ (Paris: Alcan, 1926). And in this country the work of the great historian of religion Mircea Eliade is well known, especially his _Myths, Dreams, and Mysteries_, trans., by Philip Mairet (Harper & Brothers, 1960), and _The Sacred and the Profane: The Nature of Religion_, trans. by Willard R. Trask (Harcourt, Brace & World, Inc., 1959). See the article by Douglas Allen, "Mircea Eliade's Phenomenological Analysis of Religious Experience," _The Journal of Religion_, Vol. 52, No. 2 (April, 1972), 170-186. Cf. Lauer, _op. cit._, pp. 79-81.

[57]See _The Structure of Awareness_ (Abingdon Press, 1969), p. 14, note 1, for a biographical sketch of his interests and writings.

[58] Cf. _ibid._, p. 25.
[59] Cf. _ibid._, pp. 15-20.
[60] See _ibid._, pp. 79-84.
[61] See _op. cit._, p. 413.
[62] See _ibid._, pp. 276-284; 415.
[63] See _ibid._, pp. 252-255.
[64] See _ibid._, pp. 255-259.
[65] See _ibid._, pp. 260-261, 299; 301; 303; 410-411; 415; 454-456. For an interesting critique of this approach and its differences from those of Paul Tillich's system of correlation see the article by Tom F. Driver under the section "Major Book Reviews," _Union Seminary Quarterly Review_, Vol. XXV, No. 3 (Spring, 1970), 361-367.
[66] Cf. _ibid._, pp. 261, 265-269.
[67] See _ibid._, p. 459.
[68] See The _Phenomenon of Religion_ (Herder and Herder, 1973), p. 6.
[69] See _ibid._, pp. 16; 148.
[70] See _ibid._, pp. 35; 49.
[71] Cf. _ibid._, pp. 32-34; 49; 52.
[72] See _ibid._, pp. 61-62.
[73] Cf. _ibid._, pp. 67, 70, 74, 75, 76; _et. passim_ in ch. 2.
[74] See _Body Theology: God's Presence in Man's World_ (Harper & Row, 1973), pp. 3-8.
[75] Cf. _ibid._, p. 3; also, Vogel, _Is the Last Supper Finished? Secular Light on a Sacred Meal_ (Sheed and Ward, 1968), pp. 139-140.
[76] See _Body Theology_, p. 18.
[77] See _ibid._, pp. 15-17. Vogel cites Maurice Merleau-Ponty, at this point, as saying that "here" is the key to "there." Man's understanding of his body is the key to understanding other bodies and places "beyond" man.
[78] See _ibid._, p. 18.
[79] Cf. _ibid._, pp. 20-21.
[80] Cf. _ibid._, pp. 22-27.
[81] Cf. _ibid._, 26-27; 92-97.
[82] See _ibid._, p. 29.
[83] See _ibid._, ch. 2 and ch. 5; cf. _Is the Last Supper Finished?_ pp. 63, 64, 95, 98, 101, 107-108.

INDEX OF NAMES